DURING AND AFTER CORONAVIRUS

How Online Freelance and Entrepreneurship Can Get You Through the COVID-19 Crisis

— DANA WISE —

2020

Table of Contents

YOUR CHECKLIST

WORK FROM HOME

Top ten tips for your daily productivity

This checklist includes

 The selection from 23 tips for working from home described in the book

 Daily habits for the most effective remote work

 Must have for a productive freelancer or entrepreneur

To download your checklist, click and visit the link:

rsagile.activehosted.com/f/7

INTRODUCTION

WE live in frightening times with this recent coronavirus pandemic affecting every person on this planet, and it's even worse if you're one of the millions of people who can't afford to miss a paycheck. If you have some money saved up, that may not last as long as the crisis. The exact economic impact of the pandemic hasn't been evaluated fully yet, but estimates have ranged anywhere from 6% to 20% unemployment.

The uncertainty is a big part of the problem, as the stock market has been fluctuating wildly while the world struggles to respond to the pandemic. While experts believe the markets might rebound after the crisis passes, it may be too late for many investors, along with the workers employed by companies reliant on those investors. The coronavirus may be creating the deepest and fastest economic crisis since before World War II. There is bad news everywhere you turn, but remember that the worst thing you can do is panic. Therefore, what exactly *should* you do to save yourself from economic ruin?

It may be time to rearrange our thinking about how and where we work. Some bright spots might emerge as a result of this crisis. This book will present quick and effective solutions to the problem of finding work while practicing social distancing.

You can make money quickly while isolated at home, and the following suggestions can ultimately be long-term. Even after restrictions are lifted, it will take a long time for life to return to normal.

Post-coronavirus life may be very different from what we're used to today. Those changes represent an enormous opportunity for online businesses and freelance work, which is what this book is about. This book will present information about a variety of online businesses and freelancing opportunities.

Here are a few things we know about the current crisis and
online work:

- Online work is one of the fastest growing business opportunities during the current crisis.

- It is likely to remain in very high demand, even after the crisis passes and the economy returns to normal.

- The post-coronavirus world will probably become quite different, since many companies will have likely transformed themselves; they will be far more willing to work with freelancers and startup online businesses.

This presents the best opportunity for those who are willing to engage in a new way of doing business.

If you want to be a winner and not a victim in this crisis, continue reading, as this book will change your life. It will help you explore a new way to work that will allow you more flexibility in your schedule and lifestyle. It's the perfect solution for the current crisis that can give you a competitive advantage, even after the crisis has passed. More than 4.7 million people—approximately 3.4% of the population—are currently working remotely, and that successful trend has been steadily growing within the last few years[1] (Braccio-Hering, 2020). When you include the number of people doing freelance work part-time, that figure rises to a whopping 57 million—or 34%—in the United States alone[2] (Upwork, 2019). This crisis has presented a major opportunity to jump into the remote workforce and refocus our business aspirations.

But, can you get started? Well, that is what this book will be discussing. I'll take you through the various types of opportunities available in online work and show you how to get started. We will be looking at freelance work and entrepreneurial or small business opportunities and discussing the types of work available in these various fields, required qualifications and experience, preferred jobs, trends in online entrepreneurship, and how you can build your brand online. While previous crises have meant the end of many businesses, the current one does present an opportunity for YOU to create a flexible business model and become a leader in the online business world. But why am I the one who can help you do this? Let me tell you a little about myself and my own online transformation.

Prior to going online, I was working for several larger companies. My manager was challenging me to treat my department as if it were my own company. Specifically, he wanted me to save on expenses, bring innovations, improve processes, and, generally, have an entrepreneurial mindset. I agreed with him but found it difficult to make any real changes. Maybe I was too deep in the corporate mindset—that is, I was too worried about securing my workplace and defending against risks. In any case, it wasn't working out, so I made the leap to create my own business and go remote.

Therefore, I can say that I fully understand your situation; however, you have two advantages that I did not have—one is the current crisis pushing people to stay at home and giving them time to think carefully about important things. The second advantage you have is me, and I've done what I'm about to describe to you. I know what it takes to make the change successfully, and I will take you through the process, highlight what you need to consider, and show you how to get your new lifestyle up and running.

You may think you are too shy and not assertive enough to go through the challenges this will require. I was thinking the same about myself, and it took me over a year to find my way. Another challenge I faced was that I thought I was not creative enough. I wondered what I would do, what value would I give my customers, how could I find them, and how could I make enough earnings to survive? The perspective I needed came from a friend of mine. That friend made me realize that it doesn't matter what your nature is—it only matters whether you're willing to take the risk. It's just a matter of time until you start seeing results.

I will show you how I worked everything out and how you can too. Currently, I am working five different freelancing and entrepreneur jobs—some local and some remote. I was also affected by the coronavirus crisis, but that has only proved to me how valuable it is to have built a remote business. I had to suspend some of my local onsite jobs, but because of my remote work capabilities, I am now able to continue working without disruption to my income. Since I cannot clone myself, I had to reduce some streams and prioritize others. I have made it work, and I want to show you how you can make it work too.

Working online requires a change in perspective, but these opportunities have been growing since before the pandemic. There are now even more possibilities with the global pandemic forces radically changing their lives. Consider this your opportunity to take your life into your own hands and create the future you've always dreamed about—one where you control your schedule, your talents can shine, and you can help both yourself and your loved ones navigate this brave new world.

There's no better time than right now to make the changes that will give you the freedom to do what you love and change your life for the better, while at the same time staying safe and healthy during the current crisis. This book will guide you through the many ways you can meet the challenge of this crisis and not only survive, but thrive!

Today is a great day to create your future, so let's get started!

---

[1] https://www.flexjobs.com/blog/post/remote-work-statistics/
[2] https://www.upwork.com/press/2019/10/03/freelancing-in-america-2019/

Chapter ONE

UNDERSTANDING THE THREAT OF CORONAVIRUS TO YOUR PHYSICAL AND ECONOMIC WELL-BEING

THE novel coronavirus has presented a different threat compared to what we've seen in recent years. But where did it come from, and how does it spread? It's important to understand the coronavirus to comprehend the nature of both the health and economic threat it poses in full. For that reason, I will be spending a little time discussing the origin, symptoms, health impacts, mortality rate, and economic impacts of the pandemic. It's essential to remain informed about the situation, so we can make the best decisions.

While much of the information about the coronavirus has been negative, this book will help you make positive changes to meet the challenges brought on by this pandemic. There are things you can do and control, and there is a way out of these difficult times; however, understanding the facts is key to finding a way forward. It's also important to gain as much knowledge of this experience as possible to facilitate planning for future crises. Let's start by taking a look at the origins and nature of the coronavirus.

Coronavirus and Its Origins

There are actually various forms of coronavirus, and they are all responsible for a range of illnesses—from the common cold to more severe diseases such as Middle East Respiratory Syndrome (MERS) and Severe Acute Respiratory Syndrome (SARS). The current pandemic is caused by a new strain of coronavirus, which causes an illness known as **COVID-19**. Until now, this strain was yet to be observed in humans.

Coronaviruses, along with this new one, are what are called **zoonotic diseases**, meaning they are transmitted between animals and humans. For example, SARS was originally transmitted from civet cats to humans, and MERS was transmitted from dromedary camels to humans. The current coronavirus is speculated to have originated in one of two species—bats and/or pangolins (an armadillo-like animal found in Asia and Africa).

Zoonotic diseases are common, and when you think about it from an evolutionary standpoint, it makes sense. When two species are in close contact—as with humans and animals—the virus has an opportunity to mutate and adapt to the other species, thus allowing it to have more hosts. When you're around an animal frequently, you would also be exposed to any pathogens that infect that animal—however, if that pathogen gets into you during this stage, it can't infect you. As it passes through your system often from frequent exposure, it—like any organism in a new environment—adapts. As it adapts and mutates, that is when it becomes able to infect you.

We've been around our domestic animals for thousands of years, so we've already adapted to their pathogens and they to ours; however, we haven't been exposed in the same way to those of wild animals. These animals represent a whole new reservoir of disease, making wild animal markets, such as the one in Wuhan, China, very dangerous.

Coronavirus Symptoms

The current coronavirus, which causes COVID-19, attacks the respiratory system; therefore, common symptoms include fever, cough, shortness of breath, and breathing difficulties. In severe cases, it can cause pneumonia, SARS, kidney failure, and even potentially death. The recommendations to prevent infection are one of the reasons for the social distancing, which is the primary cause of various problems in our global economy. The preventative recommendations include the following:

- Wash your hands regularly for at least 20 seconds.

- Cover your mouth and nose when coughing and/or sneezing.

- Use a protective mask and gloves when going outside.

- Cooking meat and eggs thoroughly.

- Avoid close contact with other people (social distancing).

- Avoid touching your mouth, nose, and eyes.

- Stay home if you have symptoms.

- Clean surfaces and objects that you touch regularly, such as your kitchen counter, credit card, and keys.

While people with symptoms may be the most contagious, health officials now believe that asymptomatic people may be responsible for more transmission than previously thought. That is partially why it's been so difficult for officials to get the spread of the infection under control. In addition, many people only experience mild symptoms, but they are still highly contagious[3] (Cohen, 2020).

Another factor that complicates the picture is how long coronavirus can live on surfaces. Researchers so far have observed that one strain of coronavirus can live for several hours to even days in aerosols and on surfaces. In addition, scientists at the National

Institutes of Health (NIH), the Centers for Disease Control and Prevention (CDC), the University of California, Los Angeles (UCLA), and Princeton University have all found that this new coronavirus, dubbed **SARS-CoV-2**, was detectable in aerosols for up to three hours, on copper for up to four hours, on cardboard for up to 24 hours, and on plastic and stainless steel for up to three days. Their studies have shown that, although the virus isn't naturally airborne, it can stay in the air and on droplets for several hours, and people can contract the virus after touching contaminated surfaces, even if it has been sitting on the same materials for a few days[4] (van Doremalen et al., 2020).

Coronavirus Mortality Rate

The mortality rate is another important consideration related to the novel coronavirus. Part of the problem with determining the mortality rate is that insufficient testing and mild symptoms in many people could mean that the rate of those infected has been seriously underestimated. As of this writing (March 31th, 2020), there have been 858,319 confirmed cases of coronavirus and 42,302 deaths worldwide. Taken at face value, that's a mortality rate of approximately 4%, but assessing the death rate is much more complex than that, in part because there may actually be thousands of infected people out there who have not been tested. The World Health Organization (WHO) estimates the fatality rate at 3.4%. Most experts agree that the novel coronavirus likely has a higher mortality rate than the seasonal flu, but they also believe it is not as high as what WHO estimates because of the unreported cases.

Still, regardless of the mortality rate, the proper restrictions are now in place to protect a large portion of the population. By flattening the curve of cases, the hospitals can then deal with more incoming patients. If too many infected people flood the hospitals all at once, the hospitals will be overwhelmed. Thus, the isolation and stay-at-home orders help prevent that from happening. That's why it's important that you follow the health and recommendations put forth by authorities, researchers, and WHO. Nonetheless, for all of us, there also exist economic problems. We will be taking a look at that.

The Economic Impact of Coronavirus

Given the rapid spread of coronavirus, the response from governments, businesses, and families has been variable, albeit massive and disruptive to the economy, both local and global. Though the steps taken by policymakers are necessary, the changes will have a ripple effect throughout every level of society. Here are the facts as of March of 2020:

- Though the economic markets are reacting wildly to the crisis, it has slowed down due to the global pandemic—not some core economic weakness. The economic impact of the virus is still highly unpredictable.

- The pandemic will affect all countries and almost all industries, and it has already disrupted supply chains, such as manufacturing plants that are now sitting idle. Understandably, warehouse workers are either becoming ill or staying home not to get the disease.

- The severity of the disease necessitates that the population's health and safety is the highest priority. While governments are seeking to ensure they have sufficient diagnostic, protective, and therapeutic equipment available, policymakers still need to ensure that economically vulnerable workers—in the healthcare industry and beyond—do not have to choose between working while sick and staying home. To do that, they need to make sure that workers have access to paid sick leave, paid medical leave, and family leave. That means they will need to expand current protections to enable those who are self-employed to also receive benefits.

◻ Demand is hurting more than supply; in other words, most economic disruptions have mainly impacted the demand side of the economic equation. As people are unable to go to work, they risk losing their jobs and incomes as businesses are forced to close. Additionally, businesses have had to put investments on hold amid the growing uncertainty.

◻ Exports will likely falter as countries around the world are forced to take similar actions to slow the spread of the disease.

What are Policymakers Planning to Do?

There are a number of proposals that policymakers are considering to assist with the economic impact. The main problem faced by businesses is the lack of customers and sustainable cash income that can last them for an extended period of time. That means small and medium-sized businesses will feel the impact first and more severely. Thus, economic interventions need to focus on boosting demand within the economic equation. That will likely mean replacing incomes, particularly in low and middle income families, who will be less likely to have sufficient savings to see them through the crisis.

Policymakers will, however, also have to watch and support the supply side of the economy, particularly for those businesses that are and have been hard hit by the loss of demand, like the travel and tourism industries. Uncertainty is only exacerbating the situation as businesses are reacting to not knowing how much worse it can get. Families are doing the same—they are cutting spending in fear that they will face a drastic drop in income. That's where the federal government can act to help address the uncertainty. First and foremost, Congress and the President need to be clear that they will be undertaking the necessary steps to stop an economic freefall.

Because state and local governments are on the frontline of the crisis, they need sufficient fiscal support from the federal government for securing what they need to supply public services required in their communities and support local businesses threatened by the pandemic. A factor within those communities is economic inequality, which is a problem highlighted by the current pandemic.

Income and wealth inequality create vicious cycles for lower income families. These families have lower pay; less in their savings; and fewer benefits, like health insurance and paid sick leave; to rely on during this crisis. That means they face a higher risk of infection, loss of income, along with massive health care bills. Thus, policymakers are trying to enact a number of policies to assist workers within these families. These policies include instituting moratoriums on student debt, car loans, and credit card payments.

Though the stock market has been fluctuating like crazy since the pandemic began, the focus of these policymakers need to remain on the most vulnerable in society rather than the Wall Street investors. Most people don't own stocks on Wall Street or in any other national market; thus, the ups and downs there have little impact on their personal financial health. For that reason, policymakers are negotiating cash infusions to every American, though the exact amount and timing has yet to be determined as of this writing (March 2020).

Finally, this crisis has also served to demonstrate the limit of the Federal Reserve in attacking such economic crises. While the federal government has cut interest rates aggressively to zero, those will have little effect on the economy in the short-term. The interest rates for mortgages and business loans were already low, and other interest rates, such as those for student and car loans and credit cards, have been notoriously impervious to changes in the federal funds rate.

Adding to this is how most businesses are not yet hurting for capital to invest. Tax cuts aimed at large corporations don't have the trickle down effect that policymakers might have intended, and with the last tax cut, companies simply decided not to invest the money. Therefore, any interest rate cuts will likely do little to stimulate business investment.

Help Yourself

At the moment, all any business can do is wait for the decisions of fiscal policymakers and see if these changes will help the situation. However, that might not be good enough for most workers, so what exactly can you do to help yourself? Of course, you should first make sure you are complying with the health recommendations of the experts at the CDC and your local medical centers. Getting sick will only exacerbate any economic problems you might already be experiencing as a result of the coronavirus pandemic.

If you or your family need to start saving large amounts immediately, I would recommend that you read my other book *Save Money and Spend Wisely During and After Coronavirus*. You will discover many other tips about reducing your spending instantly, helping you save money over the coming weeks and months while this crisis lasts.

Economically, however, there may be more things you can do than simply sitting in isolation at home. You can remain isolated while still taking advantage of the growing online business opportunities that will likely become more mainstream as this crisis evolves.

We will examine those opportunities for you in subsequent chapters.

Chapter Summary

In this chapter, we discussed the physical and economic impacts of the coronavirus pandemic. Specifically, we discussed the following topics:

- Coronavirus and its origins.
- Coronavirus symptoms.
- The coronavirus mortality rate.
- The economic impact of coronavirus.
- What policymakers are planning.
- How these facts can help you make the right decisions going forward.

In the next chapter, I will be showing you the general types of remote work you can do and some practical tips for working from home successfully.

---

[3] https://edition.cnn.com/2020/03/14/health/coronavirus-asymptomatic-spread/index.html

[4] Aerosol and Surface Stability of SARS-CoV-2 as Compared with SARS-CoV-1. *New England Journal of Medicine.* https://doi.org/10.1056/nejmc2004973

Chapter **TWO**

WORK FROM HOME STRATEGIES

THERE are a couple different strategies you can employ when working remotely, and you will want to explore the options that will suit your personal preferences and situation the best. It's worthwhile to review the different strategies and tips for working from home. It does require a heightened degree of self-motivation and control, as well as the need to put strong boundaries in place between your work and personal life. Let's take a look at some options and strategies for working from home.

Work from Home Options

You might not have the slightest idea of what kind of work you can do from home, but by looking at the most popular work-from-home job options, you can have a better idea of the variety of jobs that can be done remotely. Let's look at a list of the 23 most popular remote job titles as of October, 2019[5] (Howington, 2019):

Internal Services

- *Bookkeeper*—this work involves processing documents, posting entries, keeping order, preparing invoices, handling accounts receivable and payable, along with other admin tasks.

- *Accountant*—this involves analyzing books and turning that data into useful information, setting financial data structures, and helping with financial matters like preparing tax returns.

- *Engineer*—there are many kinds of engineers, such as mechanical, civil, chemical, electrical, computer, and software. Engineers use science, math, and technology to solve various problems, much of which can be done remotely. This fact is particularly true for computer/software engineers.

- *Project manager*—project managers help keep projects on track to achieve the required milestones. They also help track budgets and deadlines, delegate duties, and ensure that deliverables are completed on time. Their work is critical but does not necessarily have to be conducted in person.

- *Program manager*—program managers oversee tasks and projects that help companies achieve their business objectives. It is similar to project management, but usually involves overseeing related projects. Project managers help implement strategies and calculate the return on investment for programs and projects. It's an area of work that can easily be done remotely.

- *Interim/part-time manager*—this job requires working between 10 to 30 hours a week as a manager/leader, or during a vacancy period when the client needs to cover daily work before finding a permanent employee. These jobs may also be required to help with busy projects or during times of fast growth when the client needs to cover tasks temporarily.

25

- *Recruiter*—these people look for qualified candidates for job openings. They often write and post job descriptions, network, interview candidates, onboard new employees, and help maintain the company culture. They also approach freelancers and interim managers when the client needs those services.

Advisory and Education

- *Education*—online education has been becoming increasingly more popular over the years, and it is expected that the market will continue growing quickly. It is a successful strategy for many subject areas—teachers, tutors, and coaches can easily make use of established online educational platforms for working with students in groups or one-on-one settings.

- *Consultant*—consultants work to help companies, organizations, and individuals solve problems, find areas for improvement, and finish projects. They are individuals with expertise and experience in their field. However, for many businesses and educational fields, healthcare industries, and IT companies, consultants are a valuable part of the workforce, and they are able to do much, if not all, of their work remotely.

- *Business development manager*—business development managers can help find new business opportunities for increasing revenue. They do this by writing proposals, finding sales leads, and making sales pitches. The role requires mainly communication capabilities and networking skills. Knowledge of online marketing tools and techniques will give a greater advantage when looking for work in this field.

- *Data analyst*—this job entails interpreting various data to assist companies while they make business decisions. As part of that work, the data analyst will collect information and evaluate it for patterns. They will then compile their findings and draft reports for the company to use in the decision-making and problem-solving process.

High Demand Services

◻ *Writer*—this is one of the most common remote jobs. There are many mediums and subjects for which writers can create content, including articles, books, blog posts, emails, ad copy, and technical manuals. There are numerous online websites, newspapers, magazines, blogs, and companies that are willing to pay well for great content.

◻ *Editor*—this job entails correcting errors within written content. Editors rewrite content frequently to make it clearer, and they may also pitch ideas, provide feedback to writers, and write headlines.

◻ *UX/UI designer*—this involves facilitating the user experience and interface of a product. These individuals often create flowcharts, produce codes and scripts, and design prototyping concepts. This is another popular remote job.

◻ *Web developer*—web developers create attractive and functional websites, using their coding and graphic design skills to do so. This job usually requires expertise in HTML, CSS, JavaScript, jQuery, APIs, and frameworks built on the languages. You can work as a web developer completely from home, and there is an extremely high demand for skilled developers.

◻ *Programmers*—programmers use computer coding languages to write software and create mobile applications and websites. This is another popular remote job.

Sales and Marketing

◻ *Customer service representative*—customer service representatives are people who focus on helping customers or clients. They do this by using telephones, email, online chats, or social media to help answer questions, place orders, and resolve customer problems.

27

- *Sales representative*—these individuals sell products and services, and they also often deliver presentations and demonstrations, participate in sales meetings, and keep up-to-date on product information. Much of this work can be done remotely.

- *Account manager/account executive*—these individuals oversee client relations. They help generate sales by upselling, cross-selling, maintaining positive client relationships, and handling client communications. This is a very common remote job.

- *Territory sales manager*—this job entails developing sales prospects, creating sales strategies, maintaining customer relationships, and meeting sales goals. This is a popular remote job and is assigned typically to specific regions or territories. It also often requires travel.

Healthcare

- *Medical coder*—this job involves assigning codes to diagnoses and procedures listed on medical charts and performed on patients. People who work in this field usually work for hospitals, clinics, and/or physician's offices, but it is common for the work itself to be done remotely.

- *Nurse*—while nurses have been in demand even before the current pandemic, it is now a job that can be done remotely via telehealth platforms. This job typically requires providing assistance to patients through phone messaging, video conferencing, messaging, and/or emailing. Usually, these nurses are answering questions, instructing patients on treatments, and/or providing medical advice.

- *Case manager*—this job entails assessing patient needs, then helping find resources that they require. It can include advocating for patients, providing guidance and/or education, and building relationships with patients and their families.

This list of available remote opportunities is by no means exhaustive—these are just some of the more popular remote jobs. Other options include becoming a virtual assistant, data entry technician, administration, among other titles. Some remote jobs require education and experience, but others are entry-level with minimal requirements. There are truly many opportunities, and any sector will offer a broad range of specific jobs with countless opportunities, many of which will likely match your talents, skills, experience, and preferences.

The type of work you might be able to do will depend on your personal situation, but there is a niche among the possibilities regardless of your level of education or experience. Aside from these remote employee positions, there is also the opportunity to create your own business to meet your increasing needs. We will be discussing both freelance work and business creation in the chapters to come, but for now, we will be taking a look at a few tips from people who are successfully working from home now and how they do it.

23 Tips for Working from Home

Working from home requires a different mindset compared to otherwise because it's easy to get distracted by the familiarity of the home environment. It's also easy to procrastinate and convince yourself that you'll just work later. It is easy to procrastinate because there is no boss to tell you what to do on that specific day. That's why these tips from the people who have been successful in working from home can help set yourself up for success.

1. *Set regular work hours—even if that means at night.* You have to do what works for you, but setting specific and consistent work hours and beginning your day early will help motivate you to work. Even if you're a night owl and you plan to work at night, treat it like you would do a job to which you have to commute. **29**

Get yourself ready for work, then "go" to your office like you would with any other job.

TIP: *Write and print your schedule that will contain blocks of requirements (e.g. bring children to school), work, breaks, and other activities. Having your schedule in front of you makes the most efficient use of your time.*

2. ***Get started early.*** Working early will help you set the tone for your day and feel ready to work. This also applies even if your "morning" is at 9 PM. Some successful remote workers even put off their first meal of the day until during their first break of the day.

TIP: *Schedule your morning by allocating specific amounts of time for your routine prior to work (e.g., 8:00-8:30: showering and brushing teeth). Stick to that schedule so you can get to working as quickly as possible.*

3. ***Dedicate a space as your office.*** You really need to create a separation between your work and home life, and by dedicating a space as your office, you will accomplish that. You will also become accustomed to thinking of that space as the place to get down to business rather than for other leisure activities. Even if your "office" consists of a folding table and chair, it's actually the mental perception that matters. You will come to see that area as your office and associate it with work rather than play.

TIP: *If you have a dedicated home office space, put the name of your company on the door to make it look and feel as official as possible.*

4. ***Treat your office as if it was a real office.*** This means that you would do all the things you normally would if you were going into the office. In other words, you get up and go through your normal morning routine—shower, shave, eat breakfast, and dress for the office—and then you go to your office. The only difference should be that you have a shorter commute. Treating

work at home the same as an office will really get you into the proper frame of mind for working, which will then help you be more productive.

5. *Structure your day just like you would at the office.* When you're working from home, it will be easier to lose focus, put things off, or burn out. To prevent that, determine exactly what you need to do for the day and when you will accomplish those tasks. Use a calendar, computer program, or cell phone to schedule events and set reminders for yourself. Use the same schedule you would in the office—so, if you would normally respond to emails first thing at the office, then do the same in your home office. That will help keep you in the right mindset for work.

6. *Make it difficult to mess around on social media.* You don't want to get lost in reading through your social media, which is easy to do. To prevent that possibility, it may be a good idea to remove the social media shortcuts from your work computer or log out of your accounts. Doing so will make it harder to quickly check-in. It's also a good idea to try working in "incognito," "unavailable," or "private" mode, or whatever other mode your browser has that will tell people you're not currently available.

People on social media do not respect the need for privacy, and they often expect an immediate response. However, in this case, you are at work building your and your family's future; therefore, you need to ensure you get the privacy you need. You will need to respect your goals. The same rules apply to your private email. Remember—you're at work, and you can't browse social media if you want to get your work done, whether that is at the office or at home.

TIP: *You can turn social media on in the afternoon break for the first time, quickly respond, and close them until evening.*

7. ***Create boundaries for family members.*** Just like you, your family members or roommates who might be at home while you're working need to realize that you're working. They can't just walk into your office and disturb your flow. Make it clear that, just like at the office, they need to knock on the door and ask if it's a good time for you. If you don't set the boundaries, it will be easy for them to interrupt your work, and it will also be easy for you to get distracted. They need to understand that, just because you're working from home, it doesn't mean that you're home and available for responding to their needs. If you don't have an office door, use another signal—like headphones— to indicate to your family that you're busy.

   TIP: *Keep the door closed and put your schedule on it for family members. Agree with your family that you need to focus 100%, but during breaks, you can 100% be with them.*

8. ***Rent an office.*** For some people, it may not be possible to create an office for various reasons. Therefore, it may be a good option to rent an office nearby. You can have a shared office space with other like-minded people, which will also allow you to encourage each other when working on achieving your goals.

9. ***Work when you're most productive.*** Your motivation and energy levels will naturally ebb and flow throughout the day. Therefore, try to recognize your normal rhythms and use that knowledge to work when you know you have the energy to get more done. Save harder tasks for the time of day when you know you're at your best while saving the easier work for when you know you typically drag a little.

   Many people are most productive from early morning until lunchtime. If that's you, schedule the most important tasks for the morning. Then, designate the early afternoon to downtime, and it may ultimately be more productive to take a longer break—like a siesta. Then, after 2 or 3 pm, productivity typically increases and reaches a peak that lasts until about 6 pm. Our brain goes into a sleep mode in the night, then it will only reach about a half or third of its peak productivity compared to the morning peak.

10. *Take clear breaks.* This is important, because it's so easy to just blast through your day without stopping. However, research has shown that those who work with frequent breaks are actually more productive than those who just put their head down and work until the task is done. In fact, researchers have found that the ideal work rhythm is 52 minutes of work followed by a 17-minute break. In this study, workers remained completely dedicated to the task at hand for about an hour, but then, once they took a break, they felt refreshed and ready to dive back in for another productive hour of work[6] (Zetlin, 2020).

Additionally, there's a neurological reason for why this works. The brain works naturally in bursts of high activity for approximately one hour; after that length of time, it will switch to low activity for a while. That's when you should take a break. If you don't, your productivity will suffer. Although the research shows that if you take more breaks, your productivity will likely be reduced about once every hour, your productivity is still higher than those who work longer with no breaks. Furthermore, it's critical that you really take that break. That means disconnecting from work, getting up from your desk, and walking away from your computer. In fact, taking a walk is a great and effective way to take a break (Zetlin, 2020). And, definitely do not sit at the computer for an extended period of time.

11. *Set a time for your workday to end.* When you're working from home, it's easy to keep going, especially if you really wanted to get that task done. However, just like any other job, your workday should have a definite end time. Of course, sometimes it is necessary to work overtime, but that should be the *exception*—not the rule. Not doing so can result in burnout.

33

12. ***Commit to doing more.*** It's a great idea to overestimate how much time you'll spend doing one task, as most projects often take more time than you initially thought they would. By overestimating the length of time you'll need, you will feel more productive when you get things done more quickly. Even if you don't quite finish all the tasks you wanted to get done, you will still come out ahead after having completed a solid list of tasks. This technique can help keep you honest.

13. ***Make calls when you're alert and ready to interact socially.*** For some people, this may mean waiting until later in the day to make phone calls; however, others may feel fresher in the morning. Whatever is the case in your situation, arrange a time for making calls and other mentally challenging tasks when you feel most alert.

    If you do not need your phone for work, it's best to just turn it off completely. Even an SMS will draw your attention and distract you, and once you've broken your attention away from your work, it will take you several minutes or even hours for your brain to refocus and get back to top-level productivity. If you cannot turn your phone off, put it on silent and place it in another room. You can check it during breaks and return any important calls before you get back to work.

14. ***Focus on one task at a time.*** There's a popular misconception that multitasking increases productivity; however, the research on this specific topic says otherwise. Stanford researchers Uncapher and Wagner[7] (2018) found that heavy multitaskers performed worse than those who focused on one thing at a time. The researchers speculated the reason was because they experienced problems when organizing their thoughts and filtering out irrelevant information. The participants were also slower at switching from one task to another. Thus, the studies suggest that you'll be more productive if you work on one task at a time.

15. ***Plan your week ahead of time.*** This will reduce the amount of time you spend each day on planning. Of course, you can change your agenda if needed, but if you can commit to an agenda ahead of time, you will feel more organized and ready to go each day.

16. ***Plan tomorrow—today.*** Similar to the last task, you should plan tasks and activities for the next working day on your schedule. *Be specific*—it will help you start working on a particular task from the first minute as soon as you get into the office.

17. ***Use technology to stay connected.*** For online work, this is a *must*. There are various forms of technologies that will let you stay in touch with clients or coworkers. Programs like Zoom, Google Hangouts, Slack, and Skype make teleconferencing easy, and there's always instant messaging to communicate quickly. Be sure you have all the tools you need installed before you get started, so you don't have to deal with downloading and installing a program before you can reach out.

    TIP: *Create accounts with your business address; therefore, you will have a place where you will have only business contacts without being disrupted by friends.*

18. ***Use music or other background noises to keep you motivated while working.*** Some people like to work to music. If that's you, make sure the music suits the task at hand or is audio that won't distract you. Download your playlists ahead of time and line them up so you won't have to continue looking for songs to add to your soundtrack. If the music you are listening to is distracting (which is also my case), a good option is to have noise that will prevent other distracting sounds. You can find noise broadcasting on the internet.

19. ***Prepare your work meals in advance.*** If you prepare food for lunch or breaks in advance, you will prevent meal preparation from taking away from valuable work time. It will also **35**

keep you from having to think about what you want to eat later too.

20. ***Over-communicate with colleagues and clients.*** This is a particular concern for those working remotely. Remind those who need to know frequently about your schedule, and tell them when you have finished a task. You don't have to write an essay about it, but let them know what's happening and repeat yourself as necessary. It's easy for clients and colleagues to forget you're there when you're not in an office together, so remind them by communicating frequently. Tell them again and again about any changes to your schedule, like if you are planning to take a vacation or need a break. Doing so will help ensure there are no problems when it comes time for change.

21. ***Take sick days.*** You will want to make your work-at-home situation as similar to any other job as possible. That means you should also take time off if you're sick. If you're making your own contracts, be sure and let clients know your policy about these situations. It is really better for everyone involved if you take the time you need to heal, since working while you're sick will affect the quality of your work and your productivity.

22. ***Show up to meetings and be heard.*** It's really easy for colleagues and superiors who are not working from home to forget that your opinions count too. So, when there's a meeting and even if it's not offered, ask to be included via video conferencing. Make sure you speak up and contribute to the meeting to let people know you're there. Even if that just means saying "Hello" to everyone when the meeting is starting, speaking up will make your presence known.

23. ***Use a secured virtual private network (VPN).*** Using a VPN is a security measure you can use to protect your privacy whenever you're connected to a network you don't control. This is

important if you're ever working not just from an internet cafe, library, or airport, but also when you're accessing certain servers or websites. In case of the latter, it can help you access the information you may not otherwise be able to get. Since you are now the one who must take care of any IT problems, you'll want to make sure your computer and internet network are safe. Using a VPN whenever you need to log in with a password is a great indicator for knowing when to do that.

Once again, this is not an exhaustive list of tips to help you prepare for working at home, but it's still a great start. Working from home takes a bit more self-discipline, but these tips should help make it easier. Once you get used to your office being in your home, you'll start treating that space just like you would any other office.

Now, imagine if all employee workspaces were like this. Your boss respects that you are working on a task and they recognize that they need to wait another 17 minutes until you are available. You don't have to worry about an angry call from a colleague who sent you an urgent email—today's 7th—half an hour ago, and you have not yet taken care of what they need. You can achieve these things at home. Following my guidelines can make working from home several times more productive as compared to working at the office.

The next question is where to find those work-from-home opportunities, which is something we'll tackle in subsequent chapters.

Chapter Summary

In this chapter, we've discussed some general forms of remote work that's available. Specifically, we've covered the following topics:

- Work from home options.
- The most popular jobs for remote workers.
- 23 tips for working from home.
- Treating your home office like any other office.

In the next chapter, we will be taking a look at the definition and distinction of freelance work from contractors and traditional employment. We'll also be examining the pros and cons of each.

---

[5] https://www.flexjobs.com/blog/post/20-most-common-work-from-home-job-titles-v2/

[6] https://www.inc.com/minda-zetlin/productivity-workday-52-minutes-work-17-minutes-break-travis-bradberry-pomodoro-technique.html

[7] Minds and brains of media multitaskers: Current findings and future directions. Proceedings of the National Academy of Sciences, 115(40), 9889–9896. https://doi.org/10.1073/pnas.1611612115

Chapter THREE

FREELANCE WORK

LET'S start with the definition of a freelance worker. Typically, this is someone who offers their services for a fee, but without the expectation of a permanent, single client. Now, you might have repeated clients or clients for whom you work on a regular basis, but usually, freelance work means working from one contract to another. It's a form of self-employment that is similar to operating your own home business. Let's take a closer look at the definition of a freelance worker versus contractors and regular employees:

1. *Freelancer*—this title means you're self-employed, pay your own taxes, don't usually have your own employees, have full control over where you work, likely have several clients and projects, determine your own rates, and usually work on smaller, shorter-term projects with clients. However, with being a freelancer, you would not be receiving company benefits.

2. *Contractor*—this can apply to freelance work, as some freelancers are contractors, but it's important to note the few

distinctions between typical freelance work and that of contractors. As a contractor—like a freelancer—you generally set your own work hours, have full control over the work you take on, and you can advertise your services for new business. Also like freelancers, you are self-employed and responsible for handling your own benefits and taxes. Some contractors work through an agency—in that case, they are more similar to a regular employee.

The main difference between contractors and freelancers in how contractors tend to work on one large project with a single client at a time. Also, while contract work can happen remotely, it happens more frequently on a client's worksite or in their offices.

These two forms of self-employment differ from a regular employee in the following four ways:

◻ An employee typically works for one company permanently and gets paid regularly, whether that be hourly, salaried, on a commission, or a combination of those forms of pay.

◻ Most employees work from a company office; although, some do negotiate remote work from home on certain days.

◻ Most employees work within the confines of a contract or job description that details their salary and work hours. The company typically determines when and where the employee will work.

◻ Most employees rely on their employer to withhold the proper taxes, which are usually deducted from their wages automatically.

According to an independent study by Upwork and Freelancers Union, the majority of American workers will be full or part-time freelancers by the year 2027[8] (2017). The situation with the coronavirus may have accelerated that projection, giving you the opportunity to get in ahead of the trend. But why is freelance work so popular?

Freelance Popularity

From a corporate perspective, freelancers and contract workers give the company more agility, as these workers can respond to its needs at any given time. Full-time employees cost thousands in benefits and other expenses, even when work is slow, so hiring freelancers offers a solution to that problem. Furthermore, hiring freelance workers means the employer doesn't have to pay for idle time, such as vacations, sick leave, training, and business travel. Also, remember that the best employees are usually already working, which means the employer is left with deciding between hiring an average employee who may not be up to the challenging tasks, or hiring a star and having to overpay that person later. With freelancing, an employer can hire the perfect employee for the job description. In that way, freelancers provide added value for their clients.

Freelancing does offer the workers certain advantages, though it's important to consider the drawbacks and prepare for those as well. One of the best things about freelance work is flexible hours, which allows for a healthier balance between work and personal life. While there exists the possibility that you'll experience long periods of no work, most freelancers choose this lifestyle because they want it and find it a better fit for their current goals and needs—not because it's the last resort. Still, there are some important things to consider before deciding to freelance.

◻ **Insurance**

If you're working for an employer, they will typically have an insurance plan to offer you as a benefit, but as a freelancer, you will have to find your own insurance plan. You'll also want to provide for a retirement fund. These costs need to be part of the consideration when you bill clients. You need to break up the total cost into a per-project fee that covers your expenses.

Still, most freelancers find that they take home more money, even though they have to pay for their own benefits.

- **Freelance success mean marketing**

  Since you'll be on your own as a freelancer, you will need to prepare to market yourself and your work. You bear the burden of finding new clients and selling your talents to them, which often means a lot of unpaid work associated with prospecting, networking, winning a job offer, accounting, and various other administrative tasks. These are all unbillable hours, but they are critical for success.

  The good news is that, as you do more great work, you won't have to work as hard to market yourself. You'll develop a portfolio that will do some of the work for you. Also, word-of-mouth advertising can bring clients to your business without you having to seek them out. Once you are approached by a client, you can usually charge more than if you had to seek them out manually.

- **Flexible hours**

  Perhaps the biggest draw of freelance work, as mentioned, is the freedom to set your own hours. Though you might be working more than 40 hours per week, you can arrange those hours to suit your schedule better. One of the drawbacks to that, however, is that there is no such thing as a paid vacation. If you take time off for any reason, that means you're not making money for that amount of time. Still, with good planning, you'll find you can enjoy all the benefits of a flexible work schedule, including taking vacations without having to worry about lost wages. The most important thing to ensure is that you keep good communication with your valued clients, so they can know your availability.

◻ **Physical limitations**

For those with physical limitations, freelance work can give them the flexibility they need. In fact, 46% of freelancers are unable to work in a traditional job because of physically limiting personal circumstances[9] (Upwork, 2019).

◻ **Quick start up**

Starting out as a freelancer is affordable, quick, and relatively easy, especially when compared to other forms of self-employment. In addition, as soon as you can find a client, you can then start getting paid, which may be even faster than getting employed.

◻ **You name your price**

Freelancing doesn't come with a set salary and, of course, the work is not necessarily consistent. For this reason, you have to consider your extraneous costs carefully, which would normally fall to the employer in a traditional job. You have to keep careful track of those expenses, so you can build those costs into your estimates.

One good way to establish your freelance fees is to know exactly what the costs of running your business are and make a list for them, so you can then add a percentage to the fee for each project. You'll want to consider your standard bills like electricity, internet/phone connection, mortgage/rent, office costs including equipment (computers, software, maintenance) office supplies (paper, ink, pens, and paper clips), and any other services you pay for like domain costs, invoicing platforms, media spending, and the various add-ons related to your profession.

Once you have a list of your costs per month, you can calculate your freelance rate baseline. You can then add on a safety cushion and percentage for your profit. Another way to do it is to take your yearly gross income for a similar job, add 25% to 45% for your insurance and admin costs, the safety cushion, and profit. Then, divide that by 250 working days. Finally, divide that number by 8 hours per day working, and you will then have an estimate of an hourly fee. We'll cover this more in detail in subsequent chapters, but suffice it to say that you will have to figure out how much you want to charge clients for your services, and you will have to take these into consideration to ensure you're making enough money to live and thrive.

Comparisons— Traditional Employment versus Freelance Work

It might also help—when trying to decide on whether to become a freelancer—to look at some of the pros and cons of freelance work compared to traditional employee work. The money and lifestyle can be radically different between the two. So, is freelance work right for you, or should you stick with more traditional types of employment? The following sections will go over some considerations to consider when deciding between the two.

Steady income and benefits—this is one of the biggest arguments in favor of traditional employment. Most companies offer health insurance along with some kind of retirement planning. There is also the subject about paid vacations. Freelancers, on the other hand, do have to pay for their own benefits and won't have the benefit of paid vacations. Also, while regular employees know the wage they will be earning, freelance income can fluctuate dramatically—one month, you might be working on a couple big projects and earning double compared to the traditional employee; however, in the next month, you might only have one job that pays just a few hundred dollars upon completion.

Income potential—Freelancers have the most income potential. If you're working a traditional job, you may have opportunities for growth, but those are determined by your employer, typically with an upper limit. If you're a freelancer, you would be determining your growth opportunities, setting your own rates, and won't have any limits on your income. As long as you are good at finding clients, marketing yourself, and can complete your projects, the sky will literally be the limit for you. There are many freelancers that do their jobs so excellently that they have a full agenda with clients competing for them. As a freelancer, being great at one high-value skill can be a great asset when picking up clients.

Taxes—taxes are the needles in everyone's sides. With traditional employment, taxes are deducted from your paycheck and filing each year is usually a much simpler process. However, as a freelancer, you will be deducting business expenses, which can amount to significant savings. There are a number of things you can write off on your taxes, including a portion of your mortgage if you have a home office, the portion of your utilities that run your office, other home-related expenses, your office supplies, and any other business-related expenses. Those costs can really add up, which is why being a freelancer can be a great advantage.

Moreover, if you handle your freelance business right, you'll also be able to avoid high self-employment taxes (we'll discuss this in a later chapter). If your entire income for any given year comes from freelance work, you'll likely have to pay something in taxes, as opposed to traditional employment where most employees would receive a tax refund. So, if you choose freelance work, you will need to plan for that.

Growth opportunities—as a traditional employee, you would usually have the opportunity to climb the corporate ladder. This can allow you to increase your income and status significantly. However, such will often involve a trade-off that will impact the amount of quality time you would get to spend with your family.

Still, the path for professional growth is usually laid out clearly with traditional employment.

On the other hand, as a freelancer, you're starting out at the top of your ladder. Freelancers have more work opportunities. There is a wider variety of project possibilities to choose from, which provides the freelancer with a level of freedom that the traditional employee simply doesn't have. As an employee, you might have proven you are well-qualified and experienced for a promotion, but as long as the position is occupied, you will likely get nowhere. You may get a promise one year, but then the next year, you may get an excuse for why you were not promoted... again. In this case, you are limited only to those job positions within your company and for which you have the appropriate skills. As a freelancer, those limits don't apply, and you can give yourself a promotion at any time!

Social interactions—Traditional employees have one thing that freelancers don't: a regular group of people they see in person and with whom they can socialize. This can lead to some fulfilling work experiences and can amount to an important part of your social life. On the other hand, freelancers have more lifestyle flexibility and don't have to deal with any office politics or drama it creates. Furthermore, freelancers get to choose when and where they work, giving them the freedom to adjust their schedules around the requirements of their social lives. If you have children, freelancing can have some great flexibility benefits for you.

Even the most flexible employers can't compare to the freedom of freelance work. However, you should note before deciding on freelancing for this perk alone that this freedom can easily turn into loneliness. Freelancers have to find socializing options, like having shared offices with others or even joining a freelance professional organization or club if they want to stay healthy within the profession. Finding more people in the same niche gives you the opportunity to talk about the challenges of your work. **47**

Job security—while there is more income security with traditional jobs, the security of the job itself isn't always assured. Because the traditional employee only has one "client," they are more at risk than most freelancers who work with several clients. Even if you work in a large company, recent events such as the Great Recession of 2008 and the current Coronavirus crisis have demonstrated that traditional work may not offer as much security as one would hope. On the other hand, freelancers have multiple clients, and if they lose one, they would likely still have others to work with while they look for more. Yes, they may have to stay on their toes and fight harder for those clients, but they also learn quickly how to secure new clients and keep them. That can be better than what is often a false sense of security you would get with traditional employment.

Self-discipline—while traditional employment requires a basic level of self-discipline (getting up, getting to work on time, doing what you're expected to do, etc.), freelance work takes that requirement to a whole new level. Freelancers have to be self-starters and always looking for the next job.

As a freelancer, you have to become comfortable with marketing yourself, winning over clients, drumming up your business, and making sure you get paid. You're much more likely to get rejected as a freelancer than with traditional employment, and that uncertainty can definitely become a source of stress.

So, what is right for you? In these uncertain times, we've definitely seen the drawbacks of relying on traditional forms of employment. However, if your company is amenable to the idea, it might be a good compromise for you if your job allows you to work from home. This is not a solution, however, for employees for whom telecommuting or working at home is not an option, such as wait staff and other service industry employees. For those individuals, it might certainly be worth taking a chance as a freelancer.

The best thing you can do to decide is to be honest with yourself about your personality—are you self-disciplined and self-motivated? Are you attentive to details? Do you value flexibility over steady employment? If you can answer yes to these questions, then freelance work might be just the right fit. The following list contains a few more points to consider as you make your decision:

- Freelancer work can be more enjoyable because it provides only value to the client. On the other hand, employees spend a significant portion of their time reviewing company emails and attending meetings that may not be directly relevant to their work.

- It is often difficult to get a good job as an employee. Interview questions may include why were you terminated from a previous job or why you left, which can be difficult to answer. Freelancers are simply hired based on their portfolio of previous work.

- Salaries are fixed expenses that increase when a new employee is hired. Freelancers offer great flexibility to clients and can agree on an hourly fee, and more work (expenses) is related to revenue increases, meaning that hiring freelancers is always profitable.

- As an employee, you can be overeducated for the job and underpaid.

- During crises, employers reduce both staff and salaries. If the employee has any option, it is to choose between staying with a lower salary or searching for another employer, neither of which is optimal.

- When the client's business declines, the freelancer can already be contracting for more work from other clients.

- It is more costly to live as an employee because of various factors like commuting expenses or buying lunch every day.

49

- Many managers are position leaders, and it can often be stressful and discouraging to work in those conditions. As a freelancer, you would only have to deal with the product/service you are delivering, and you wouldn't have to account for the actions of others.

This chapter should have given you some good information to consider in terms of the benefits that can come with freelance work. Informed decisions usually produce the best results!

Chapter Summary

In this chapter, we discussed freelance work definitions, along with its pros and cons. Specifically, we've covered the following topics:

- Freelancer definition.
- Contractor definition.
- Traditional employee definition.
- Growing freelance popularity.
- Freelance work benefits.
- Freelance work as compared to traditional employment.

In the next chapter, we will be talking about what it takes to get set up as a freelancer.

---

[8] https://www.upwork.com/press/2017/10/17/freelancing-in-america-2017/
[9] https://www.upwork.com/i/freelancing-in-america/

Chapter FOUR

HOW TO GET SET UP AS FREELANCER

SETTING up freelance work can be really easy to do—it takes less than a day and requires little to no cash upfront. You can start working as a freelancer simply and without creating a business entity, but there are some important considerations if you choose that path. First of all, if you don't create a business entity, you will, by default, be considered a sole proprietorship with unlimited liability. The most significant consideration with this fact is that, if you're sued, your personal assets will be at risk.

Additionally, without a business entity, you will face much higher self-employment taxes. Therefore, it's highly recommended that you create a **limited liability company** (LLC). Doing so shields your personal assets from a lawsuit, and in the event you lose and cannot pay, the company can be dissolved. However, before we get too deep into that, let's just start at the beginning. You've decided, like more than 56 million US citizens[10] (Stolzoff, 2018), that freelancing is right for you. How do you begin?

Step #1: Define Your Goals

The first thing you want to do is to define your measurable goals clearly. Without that, you'll find yourself faltering at the outset. You don't want just to set your ultimate goal; you need to describe the steps it will take to get there clearly. Begin by answering the following questions:

- Is freelancing going to be your primary source of income or just a side job; or, will it just be a way to get through the current crisis?

- Are you using freelancing as a stepping stone to some other goal?

- Do you want to do freelance work because of the lifestyle benefits associated with being your own boss?

Regardless of your goals, make them abundantly clear. For example, your goal might be to be fully self-employed through freelancing. Otherwise, your goal could be associated more with doing something you truly love. Whatever your goals are, write them down in as much detail as you can. Don't just say, "My goal is to get rich;" instead say, "My goal is to make a minimum of $100,000 per year with freelance work."

Please remember that goals should be specific with regard to what you want to do, how much you want to wear, and when you want to achieve that level of income. You may be wondering about the possibility of your goals changing. You are right—they not only might change, but it's also almost certain they will. That's okay because, as you move through the process, you'll find alternatives that will suit you better. However, if you start with vague goals, those will likely lead nowhere and you'll have difficulty measuring any progress you're making.

Along these same lines, you will want to decide on the exact kind of freelance work you will be doing. Will you be writing, designing, **53** or developing something? What kind of work will you be doing? Once you have clarity around that, you can then begin to outline shorter-term goals and benchmarks that will help get you closer to your ultimate goals.

Let's look at an example—you have a goal to be fully self-employed as a freelance worker because you want to set your own hours, decide who to work with, and call your own shots. The next question is: how do you get there? One of the first steps, regardless of the type of freelance work you want to do, is to get your income up to a sustainable level prior to quitting your day job. During this coronavirus crisis, you may not have the luxury of doing that, but if you do, it's advisable to wait to quit your job until your freelance income is at least 75% of what your job is paying you.

Without that luxury, you'll have to dive right into freelance work to start earning a paycheck as quickly as possible. You can do that, but you would still need to lay out your income target for freelance work, along with some realistic expectations in terms of how much time you will have to devote to your freelance jobs and the income they will bring you. To calculate your needs, add up all of your living expenses, including the things you want to be able to do, but can't do currently based on your present income. Then, add a security cushion and a profit margin, which should give you a rough idea of the income you need to sustain yourself. Once you do all that, you're finally ready for the next step.

Additionally, you should remember that a great advantage of being a freelancer is saving on expenses. You're staying at home and saving on travel expenses, along with other kinds of expenses such as restaurants. This amounts to hundreds of dollars every month.

If you would like to learn more about personal finances for free-lancers, check out the other book I wrote, *Save Money and Spend Wisely During and After Coronavirus*. You will learn even more practical tips to start saving hundreds a month from today.

Step #2: Research the Industry

You want to do a little market research in the area of free-lancing in which you're hoping to work. Who are your customers and competitors? What can you offer your clients that the competition can't? Is there something different that you do in that niche that your clients will appreciate? Try to find how you are different from the majority. Are you faster, lower in cost, or unique in anything you provide?

Also, do a little research into what your competitors are charging. You don't want to try to charge less than all of your competitors, but you want to price yourself somewhere in the middle. The point you'll make to the client is that you offer quality services that are worth the price, even if that price is higher than other freelancers offering the same thing. You can always list your services on freelance work sites, but you will likely be paid less than what you're worth. However, to start earning some money and getting your name out there, freelance work sites are great options that will be described later in the book.

Researching the industry is also important for finding a profitable niche. By doing that, you'll be competing on value rather than price. For example, rather than simply taking any and all graphic design projects, concentrating on one profitable niche, such as infographic design for startup blogs, will help you deliver real quality for your clients better, and your clients will appreciate—and pay for—those kinds of services. Doing so will also allow you to choose a niche that truly interests you, which will serve to keep you motivated as well. Along with that, while most successful freelancers start with just one specific service, if you are great at other related fields, you can also offer those services to your satisfied customers.

Step #3: Establish Your Business Entity

As we've mentioned, you can work as a freelancer without a business entity, but such is really not advisable, particularly if you plan to make this venture a permanent change. There are four ways you can structure your business entity:

- Sole proprietorship
- Partnership
- Limited Liability Company (LLC)
- Corporation

Most freelancers opt for a sole proprietorship as, as previously discussed, this is the default if you don't register with the state. However, as also discussed, the problem with this option is that, with a sole proprietorship and a partnership, your personal assets are at risk if you are sued. That's because, with these entities, there's no separation between you and the business, which is all why an LLC, S-Corp, or C-Corp might be the better choices. With these entities, you are the owner of the business and, if someone wants to sue, they would be suing the business rather than you.

LLC and corporations offer limited liability, so if you are sued, your personal and family assets would stay safe. An important difference between the forms, however, is that they are taxed differently. C-Corps must pay corporate taxes, whereas LLCs and S-Corps are what are called *pass-through or tax disregarded entities*. Their profits are passed through to the owner, who can then report gains and/or losses on their personal tax returns.

With C-Corps, the corporation pays taxes, and any dividends paid to shareholders—which would include you as the owner— would be taxed as well. Because of this "double taxation" potential, many business owners prefer to go with an S-Corps or LLC. However, new laws have reduced the tax burden on C-Corps, and that fact, along with the other benefits of C-Corps—such as insurance options—might make it the better option. Before creating your business entity, you might want to take the time to consult with an accountant to see what will work best for you.

Step #4: Identify Your Clients

To really be effective as a freelancer, you will have to identify your target clients. When you're first starting out, you might take any clients who will hire you, but you would really want to think about who will benefit the most from your services. Who are the right clients for your freelance work? Thinking about this consideration will help you to target your marketing better to those who are most likely to need you. Also, once you've landed a few clients in your focused niche, it's likely the word will get around to other potential clients about your services, which can bring clients to you instead of you having to go search them yourself.

Focusing in on specific clients can be a difficult decision to make because you might have to turn away much needed business; however, once you narrow down your target clients, you will have better success in the long run. If you begin with a few clients who really like your work, that momentum can pick up quickly. Focusing on your target clients also allows you to produce higher quality work and compete on value rather than price. Happy clients then become your sales force, which can help you become the go-to resource in your niche. It will also allow you to charge clients premium rates for your services.

To determine your ideal client, ask yourself the following questions:

- Who will find my services useful?

- Will my clients be larger corporations, smaller businesses, or individual clients?

- Where are they located?

- Why will they find my services valuable?

- Who can afford to pay what I charge?

- Who, within the business, makes the decisions about hiring freelance work?

- Can I find a way to connect with them on a personal level?

Be specific in answering these questions, so you can define your typical client. Once you have this information, you can create a cold email (unsolicited email) that cuts to the core needs of your ideal clients, helps you connect with them, and allows you to offer them an immediate value. If you try to be everything to everybody, you will get nothing. If, on the other hand, you choose a very narrow niche of customers, you can make a quick breakthrough and become very attractive to that small group of clients.

If you have a favorite restaurant, why is that? Usually, it's because they have something that suits you well. It can be a specific food, waiter, the space, music, or the other guests you meet there. As long as the restaurant continues with what you like, you will be their regular customer. Even if the restaurant does not have a lot of other customers, it can still be successful with a small and select group of satisfied customers. That is exactly what you want to do—build a select group of satisfied clients who will use your services regularly.

If you're not sure how to identify your ideal client, study your network of prior employers, previous clients, or even suppliers for your previous boss. You could also observe a good colleague or friend who epitomizes your perfect client. Think about it this way—if you were telling your best friend about your services, which friend would you choose, and what benefits would you tell them about in terms of what you're offering?

Step #5: Set Strategic Prices

There are a number of helpful websites out there that can assist you when trying to decide how much you want to charge. The first thing to remember is that you are not pricing your services based on what your competitors are charging; rather, you want to charge your services based on the quality and value you provide your clients. Part of setting your prices will depend on the type of clients you're targeting.

Really, there is no such thing as prices that are too high—they may be too high for the clients you're targeting, but there are some clients out there for whom they will not be too high. Therefore, you need to do your homework and find out the price range of the clients you want to target. Then, you can pitch your services to them at a price they can justify because of the quality and value of work you provide. One thing about pricing—many freelancers find that the more they charge, the less clients complain, and you can choose to offer your services to clients with bigger budgets.

The other thing to remember about pricing is that you need to make sure you charge enough to cover your living expenses, along with a decent profit. Here's one way you can calculate an hourly rate:

- Begin with your target annual salary—for example, $75,000 per year.

- Factor in your new expenses and overhead as a self-employed freelancer—let's say, another $22,513. That would mean that your new adjusted annual income will be $97,513.

- Determine your billable hours per year—the number of working hours per year is 2,080, but you would probably want to do freelance work to have a more flexible schedule and more time off. So, with three weeks of vacation, 7 US annual holidays, and 5 sick days, that would come to 216 hours fewer, or 1,864 hours.

But, that's not all—you have to account for the non-billable hours that you would be spending searching for new clients, responding to emails, and other administrative types of work. A good rule of thumb is to allow for 25% of your hours to be spent on non-billable activities. That would mean 1,864 multiplied by .75, which equals 1,398 billable hours per year.

- Last, divide the adjusted annual salary (in this example, $97,513) by the adjusted billable hours per year of 1,398. That would come down to $69.75 per hour, and it's okay to round that up to $70 per hour.

Once you have an hourly rate, you can determine what you would charge for salaried work or by contract much more easily. You need to be ready with different pricing models for various projects or clients. The pros of the hourly rate are that clients are familiar with the concept, and it is the most common pricing model for freelance work. Also, it's easy to keep track of your hours using various time-tracking programs that are already readily available. Moreover, hourly rates are easy to negotiate. You know the hourly rate you need to charge for your desired annual income, and from there, you can pre-define an expedited services rate quite easily. Lastly, pricing per hour gives you more flexibility with the client, particularly if they continue to try adding extra services they want you to complete. It's much easier to adjust and negotiate pricing in this scenario if you're using an hourly rate model because they would be paying for that extra time.

The drawbacks of the hourly model stem from how clients will often want to know the total price of a project. Even a few hundred dollars difference in costs can make a huge difference for small business clients. Also, if you put your hourly rate on your website, it will give you less negotiating power for more complex or demanding projects. Finally, you will be penalized by hourly rates if you're fast, and delivering high-quality services quickly should be a well-paid attribute rather than a penalty.

Another type of pricing model is known as a monthly retainer, which is usually used by more experienced and established free-lancers. With this model, the client would pay you on a recurring basis and in advance. You get a fixed amount each month, regard-less of whether you worked for the client that particular month. Essentially, they're paying to have you there when they need your services. This can be good for both sides, but it can also go bad quickly. To use this model, you need to have a clear agreement on what projects are included in your retainer price, and what services might incur additional fees. This information would be stated plainly in a contract that both parties would sign.

The benefits of a monthly retainer are that you would receive steady pay, which can help both you and your client feel safe in the contract. The client gets a significant advantage as well, since they have you on retainer, so you're available for the agreed-upon work. They also don't have to pay overhead costs as they would for an employee. However, the drawbacks include how the client will think of your services as on-demand, and they'll expect an imme-diate response from you whenever they need. That can feel a lot like a boss. Also, just as your client comes to be dependent on you, you may come to depend on their monthly check, which can be a problem if you lose that client for any reason. Thus, even in this situation, you would still have to prioritize getting more clients, and doing so can be difficult because you would have less time for other clients.

Another model would be a contract-by-contract basis for your freelance work. That can give a steady income over the course of the contract, but there are a lot of considerations for how to design that contract. For example, for particularly long-term projects, you'll want to get paid for meeting certain milestones so you won't have to wait until the contract has ended to get paid. Of course, for setting the entire price of the contract, you will have to estimate your hours in advance, which can be tricky if you don't have a good grasp on how long it will take you to do the job.

One way to get around this problem is to set an hourly rate as part of the contract, along with an estimated time to complete the work. Once you do that, you can then include a clause that states, in essence, that work that goes above and beyond the estimate will incur additional labor costs. That gives you some leeway; however, you would really need to make sure you do a good job of estimating the time it will take you to do the work. Enacting that "additional costs" clause should be the exception, not the rule.

Another good pricing strategy is to set a low price for the basic product, then you can add extra costs for additional work. For example, a designer can charge for one proposal with one revision, then offer more designs and revisions for an extra cost. This pricing would likely appear fair to clients because they know what they are paying for and can choose different packages. The benefits of this model for the client include how they would gain a better estimate for the total cost of the project.

It's also important to understand that there are certain types of jobs in which specific pricing models would work. For example, no client would pay a designer or a web developer hourly because they cannot control how intensively the freelancer is working. On the other hand, jobs like a virtual assistant, medical assistant, or telephonist would normally be paid based on time. Before you set your pricing strategy, it's helpful to research what pricing methods are used most often in your field of choice.

In the end, if you start out using one pricing model, then find it isn't helping you reach your desired income, there are alternatives. You can change the model you use or vary your model based on the client. You're not necessarily locked into one model—just be sure to indicate that there are different pricing models depending on the client needs indicated on your website and in your promotional materials and offers.

Step #6: Set Up a Website

Now that you have identified your ideal client and established your pricing model(s), it's time to set up a website with that client in mind, so you can communicate the services you're offering effectively. With your business entity established—or at least, your business name—it's a good idea to go ahead and buy a domain name for your website. They are often fairly and reasonably priced (usually starting from $1 per month), and they help clients remember where they can go to find you. You'll want to think carefully in terms of naming the website, and you can incorporate your business name with your specialty, such as BostonBlogWriter.com.

Once you have a domain name, you can set up a high-quality website. One thing you can try with your website is create a portfolio containing services you offer. Remember—this is the first impression that many potential clients will have of you, so you need to show good communication, display exactly what your services are for, who they are for, and why you are the best person for the job. Be short and to the point because people do not read websites; they scroll through them with eyes and notice visuals, bold words, and only the information they need. To be effective, your freelance portfolio website will need to contain the following items:

- A description of your services and specialties, along with specific examples of your work.

- Your contact information.

- An email subscriber link.

- Your relevant skills, education, and accomplishments.

- Client testimonials—if you don't have any, you can ask former or current coworkers or bosses to provide testimonials of your work.

- Regular updates that show your evolution, new clients, and updates of your sample work.

In addition to these items, you also want your website to show off a bit of your personality. Be professional albeit true to yourself. Check out other freelance websites to get some ideas and inspiration on how to position yourself in your niche. If you can afford to do so, it might also be worth your while to hire a web designer. There are a number of freelance pages where you can find great freelancers for web page development for some low prices. Your website is not something to skimp on, so getting a professional web designer can really help make your website look and feel official. There is a certain psychology behind building a website in a way that will make others trust it and you, and it's important to understand that while designing your website[11] (Kachan, 2019).

Step #7: Take Care of Business

There are a couple things you'll want to do as a newly established, self-employed worker. First, you'll want to make sure you have all the required business licenses pertaining to your profession. In some locations, even freelancers are required to have business licenses. You don't want to get caught having to pay a penalty because you didn't have the proper city, county, or state licenses, so check those out for your area and make sure you're in compliance.

Next, it might serve you well to get an Employer Identification Number (EIN). An EIN is helpful for business documents and if you should find yourself needing to hire or outsource work for a project. It also helps keep your social security number from becoming vulnerable to theft.

Another thing you'll probably want to do is open a bank account for your business. It's really smart to keep your business and personal bank accounts separate, as doing so will help with accounting when tax time comes around, so that you can know how much you earned from your business better. Choose a bank that specializes in small businesses and offers good packages for reasonably low prices.

Step # 8: Set Up Profiles on Freelance Job Sites

This is one way to find freelance gigs. There are a number of freelance work sites, such as Upwork, Freelancer.com, among others where you can create a profile that caters to the clients you're looking to find. By creating a profile, you can both apply for jobs and receive offers from clients who have seen your profile. This may not be your main source of work, but it can get you started and give you some valuable experience. We will be discussing these freelance job sites more in the next chapter—just remember that this can be a good way to pick up side jobs after you've secured a few steady clients.

Step #9: Marketing

Even before officially launching your freelance business, you'll want to make sure you have laid the groundwork for marketing **65** your work. You want to create social media profiles everywhere you think your ideal clients spend time. It's also worthwhile to go ahead and write several blog posts so you can give that audience plenty of content to explore. Plus, it's helpful to have several blog posts in a queue and ready to publish so you can send out new messages inviting potential clients to read your latest blog posts. When clients read valuable posts, they will think, "This free-lancer seems really knowledgeable about this topic, I want to hire them." Having them ready means that, once everything else is ready, you can just post and send out messages without having to do extra work.

You'll also want to link your messages and ads to examples of your work, along with your pricing structure and contact information. It's also helpful to go ahead and get familiar with an email marketing software, so you can use it once you have an email subscriber list. If you feel comfortable doing so, you can also reach out to your personal network to market your start in this new free-lance career. Let others know you would appreciate any business referrals they might provide. As part of a marketing strategy, it might also be helpful to brainstorm with other freelancers or even partner with them to get more business. You can also barter your services for theirs.

Step #10: Plan Your Launch

You want to start out with a bang, so to speak, by creating buzz around the launch of your new freelancing career. You can start a Facebook Live video, create flyers, use a direct mail campaign, or offer some promotions on your opening day, for example. You can also offer discounts or something like, "Two free blog posts if you buy 10!" if one of your main gigs is writing blog posts. Do what you can to get people interested in what you're offering and create some incentives that can help push them in your direction. Once you've hooked some clients in, you have to deliver on the goods. It's also good to offer occasional promotions even after your launch, which can help generate new clients while maintaining those whom you have already established.

Chapter Summary

In this chapter, we discussed how to get started as a freelancer worker. Specifically, we went over the following topics:

- Defining your specific goals.
- Finding your niche.
- Establishing your business entity.
- Identifying your clients.
- Setting strategic prices.
- Different price models.
- Setting up a website.
- Taking care of business by getting any required licenses, opening a bank account, and getting an EIN number.
- Setting up profiles on freelance job sites.
- Marketing.
- Planning your launch.

In the next chapter, we will be discussing remote work examples and various sites you can use for remote work.

[10] https://qz.com/work/1441108/the-us-now-has-more-than-56-7-million-freelance-workers-and-they-vote/

[11] https://www.business2community.com/web-design/psychology-in-web-design-exploring-hidden-influences-on-users-decision-making-02200931

Chapter FIVE

REMOTE WORK EXAMPLES AND SITES

NOW that you've decided to become a freelance worker, it's helpful to discuss some specifics about freelance work and job sites. One of the most common questions is about where to find good paying freelance work.

Finding Well-Paying Freelance Work

Many freelancers can earn $90,000 per year or more. In fact, among the more than 15 million full-time freelance workers, over 3 million are earning over $100,000 per year[12] (Braverman Rega, 2019). There is also an increasing demand for highly skilled freelance workers. With nearly 60 million Americans engaging in either full-time or part-time freelance work, the market is now getting quite competitive. Still, if you're looking to make good money, you might want to consider the following highest paying job categories for freelance work, identified by Upwork (Braverman Rega, 2019):

Income of $150,000+ per year

- *Corporate law*—examples in this category include intellectual property attorneys and corporate legal counsel. Individuals working freelance in corporate law make an average of $85 per hour with a potential annual income of $170,000 or more.

- *Contract law*—positions within this niche include litigators, general counsel, and attorneys who draft contracts. These freelance workers earn an average of $75 per hour with a potential income of $150,000 per year.

Income of $100,000 to $150,000 per year

- *Financial planner*—examples in this category include experts in financial modeling, CPAs, and financial estate-planning attorneys. These individuals make an average of $62.50 per hour and have a potential annual income of $125,000 per year.

- *Management consulting*—this category includes business consultants, and they make an average of $60 per hour with a potential annual income of $120,000 per year.

- *ERP/CRM software*—solution architects, consultants, and software developers are examples in this category. These individuals also make approximately $60 per hour and can make up to $120,000 per year.

- *Network and system administration*—network architects and IT administrators can make up to $120,000 per year with an average hourly wage of $60.

- *Data visualization*—examples in this category include developers, programmers, data visualization analysts, and survey and research design consultants. These individuals make approximately $50 per hour and can earn as much as $100,000 per year.

- *Machine learning*—deep learning analytics consultants and predictive analytics consultants are examples in this category. These individuals also make around $100,000 per year and have an average hourly wage of $50.

- *Quantitative analysis*—professors of economics and statistical analysts are two examples within this category. These individuals make an average hourly wage of $50 with an annual earning potential of $100,000.

- *Presentations*—examples here include presentation designers and writers, and this is another category where the average hourly wage is $50 and the annual earning potential is $100,000.

- *Database administration*—examples here include data engineers and systems engineers, also with an average hourly wage of $50 and an annual earning potential of $100,000.

- *Display advertising*—examples in this category include graphic designers and internet marketers. The hourly wage is $50 and the potential annual rate is $100,000.

- *Email and marketing automation*—examples for this category include marketing experts, developers, senior marketing strategists, and consultants. The hourly rate is typically $50 per hour and the annual earning potential is $100,000.

- *Marketing strategy*—titles in this category include digital marketing consultants, copywriters, and B2B marketing specialists. The average hourly rate is $50 per hour with an annual earning potential of $100,000.

- *Search Engine Marketing (SEM)*—one example in this category is Google AdWord experts, and it also has an average hourly rate of $50 per hour with a potential annual rate of $100,000.

- *Desktop software development*—sample titles in this category include full-stack senior web developers and customer software developers. This niche has an average hourly rate of $50 per hour with an annual earning potential of $100,000.

- *E-commerce development*—examples in this category include developers, online marketing and e-commerce solutions experts, and e-commerce integration and automation consultants. This category also has an average hourly rate of $50 per hour with an annual earning potential of $100,000.

- *Mobile developer*—sample careers in this category include iOS developers, Android developers, and mobile app developers. This category has an average hourly rate of $50 per hour and an annual earning potential of $100,000.

Income of $90,000 to $100,000 per year

- *Scripts and Utilities*—the examples of careers in this category include Google Sheets experts, apps scripts experts, and Excel automation specialists. This category has an average hourly rate of $49 per hour with an annual earning potential of $98,000.

- *Physical design*—sample careers in this category include industrial design engineers, product developers, and global visual merchandising managers. This job category has an average hourly rate of $45 per hour with an annual earning potential of $90,000.

- *Mechanical engineering*—titles in this category include mechanical engineers, structural engineers, and designers. The average hourly rate for this category is $45 per hour with an annual earning potential of $90,000.

- *Product design*—sample careers in this category include user-experience consultants and product designers. The average hourly rate is $45 per hour with an annual earning potential of $90,000.

◻ *Web and mobile design*—careers in this category include web and mobile app developers and user-experience designers. The category has an average hourly rate of $45 and an annual earning potential of $90,000.

◻ *Web development*—sample careers in this category include full-stack web development, business systems experts, user-experience designers, and front-end developers. The hourly rate average is $45 per hour and the annual potential is $90,000.

◻ *Resumes and cover letters*—titles in this category include professional development writers, career coaches, and cover letter and LinkedIn support. The category has an average hourly rate of $45 per hour with an annual earning potential of $90,000.

These job categories were pulled from categories with more than 1,000 completed jobs between January 1, 2018 and December 1, 2019 (Braverman Rega, 2019). As you can see, none of the categories here have an annual income under $90,000, and these jobs have a variety of experience and educational requirements. Within some categories, experience alone could easily land you the job, whereas others may require more advanced education.

Regardless of the requirements, these job categories and their income potentials demonstrate that a successful and lucrative freelance career is not only possible, but becoming increasingly more common. While these categories represent the top earners, there are many more freelance jobs with an average income range that allows for comfortable living. But what about the freelance sites where you can find work? Let's look at a few of the better websites that help pair freelancers with employers.

Freelance Websites

Freelance websites are platforms that pair clients with freelancers. It's a handy way to get started in the gig economy, and it can help you grow your portfolio while you are first setting up your website online. You should still do whatever it is you need to do to get your freelancing career on track (getting appropriately educated, investing in the equipment you need, getting your branding in place). Once you do, you can then start working immediately by using these websites.

A great advantage of freelance websites is that they set rules about which freelancers and clients they will accept, reducing the time and costs associated with agreeing to specific conditions with your clients. The websites often check clients and freelancers to remove any scammers. They secure payment of fees usually in a way where the client pays the website; then, after confirming the product was delivered at the agreed quality level, the amount is released to the freelancer. This payment is often much faster than if the freelancer were in direct contact with the client. In case of disagreement, the website may act as a negotiator. Some websites charge fees to one or both parties; however, these fees are often well worth the benefits provided by the website.

Next, let's look at some of the better websites for finding freelance work!

General Freelance Work

These websites have a broad sampling of freelance jobs, regardless of your specialty area. There are jobs listed for virtually any kind of service you can provide.

◻ FlexJobs.com

This is a well-curated site that includes freelance and remote jobs. It also includes other types of gig work. The curators research the jobs and monitor new gigs thoroughly, so you don't have to worry about scam postings. However, regular access to jobs on this site is not free. Still, it might be worth the investment for your niche and, if you start earning immediately, it can pay for itself.

❑ SolidGigs.com

This is a great site for finding freelance jobs fast. The SolidGigs team combs through numerous freelance job boards, and they send you the best 2% of jobs every week. Screening these jobs helps you because, otherwise, you would be doing that work. Therefore, the hours you would spend looking for the right job opportunities could then be spent pitching yourself or working. This site also has an enormous resource library you can take advantage of, including courses, interviews, templates, scripts, and other tools that can help you land more freelance work. Similar to the last, this site is not free, but it's a good investment to get both weekly gigs tailored to your niche and training resources.

❑ Fiverr.com

This site takes its name from its design—every job starts at $5. That may sound low, but you can set up tiers that go above that base $5 option, and it all can add up fast. This site is a great way to get started immediately and build your portfolio. You will find this site attractive if you plan to offer standard products and services, such as a book cover design. Many small clients prefer this site because they can search the product or service category, compare freelancers' portfolios and prices, and make the entire purchase within a few minutes.

❑ Upwork.com

Upwork was the combining result of two leading freelance job platforms—oDesk and Elance, and is now a huge job site. Upwork posts over 12 million freelancers, 5 million clients, and close to 3 million jobs each year. Thus, no matter your niche, you can find a job listed on this site. However, you have to consider that Upwork takes between a 5-20% cut from your earnings. You may also need to purchase points called connects that are required for applying for a job. One application costs between 30 and 90 cents, which is actually a good rule because it prevents certain freelancers from applying for every job. The jobs listed here are generally lower-priced; despite that, this is still the largest freelance platform in the world, and Fortune 500 businesses, along with other fast-growing startups, all use this platform to find freelancers.

◻ **Indeed.com**

Indeed collects all kinds of job openings and puts them in one place. The site is easy to search through, with features to filter remote or on-site jobs. The best parts about this site are that it's free and you can place your resume on the site and apply quickly with a single click of a button.

◻ **Guru.com**

This site makes it easy to create a profile that will show off your experience, which will make it easier for potential employers to contact you. There are also a massive amount of job postings every day, they allow you a decent amount of free applications, and they only charge a 9% commission.

◻ **TopTal.com**

TopTal works exclusively with the best—top 3%—freelance software developers, designers, finance experts, product managers, and project managers in the world. They also work with the top companies looking to hire them. TopTal has a rigorous screening process; however, once you're in, you have a greater chance of landing high-paying jobs. Building a career on TopTal will skyrocket your experience because you will be working on the most important projects from leading companies.

Writer Freelance Websites

If you're a writer, these sites will help you find jobs specific to your niche. They will help you find the clients so you can spend more time working on your craft.

□ **Contena.co**

Contena provides a huge volume of well-paid jobs for writers, editors, and content creators of almost any kind. This site features a mix of freelance and full-time remote jobs, including relatively high paying jobs. One recent example was a $10,000 per month gig writing technical ebooks. The site boasts literally thousands of other opportunities across many industries involving trustworthy companies.

□ **FreelanceWritingGigs.com**

The name of this site pretty much says it all. Freelance-WritingGigs is a well-curated job board that gets updated twice a week—on Monday and on Friday—with some great new clients who pay well for writing.

□ **PubLoft.com**

This is a great place to find solid and well-paid freelance jobs from reliable clients. Additionally, with how the site is set up, you never have to actually interact with the client. The site promises that they will help ensure that freelancers won't have to find, sell, or manage their customers, and the gigs are well-paid too. The rates start at $150 per post, and the site will also help you strengthen your writing along the way, giving you plenty of room to work on your craft without the headaches of client management.

□ **BloggingPro.com**

Despite the name, you can find all kinds of different writing gigs on this site and even help other people start blogging. The site aggregates the best writing jobs, so it's easy to find and search through the site. This site is also completely free, which is a great plus!

- **Contently.com**

  This is a high-quality, agency-style platform that connects you directly with clients for some very well-paid freelance writing projects. Some clients pay as high as $600 to $1,600 per article depending on the length and scope. Clients usually come from the most successful brands and startups in the world. The catch, however, is that you must create a portfolio first, then their account management team will hand-select you for work. Still, the site provides solid freelance advice, and you receive a free portfolio as a creative freelancer.

- **FreelanceWriting.com**

  This is an easy one—you just sign up and they send you an email everyday with the latest freelance writing jobs. The best part is that it's totally free.

Designer Freelance Websites

These are the best websites for freelance design work where you get paid for excellent work without spending much time looking for jobs.

- **99Designs.com**

  This site has an interesting format—instead of publishing a job advertisement, the client would publish a contest. Designers submit their work as an application, the client chooses the one they like best, and that designer gets paid. The downside is that, if you don't win the contest, you don't get paid. However, you can still build up your portfolio using that work.

□ **Behance.net**

This isn't exactly a freelance job site, but it's still important because it helps designers showcase their work. By setting your work up on this site and choosing the right keywords, your work will come up higher in search engines when clients are looking to hire. The site is better than a personal website for showcasing your work and, for that reason, it's important to make use of it as a way to bring clients to you. Another benefit of this site is that you can receive feedback from other designers and potential clients on your work.

□ **Angel.co (AngelList)**

If you want to work for a startup company, then AngelList is for you. Startup companies of all kinds regularly search for talent on AngelList, and it can also help you to get your foot in the door for long-term employment.

□ **ArtWanted.com**

If your niche is graphic design or digital illustration, then you can put your work on this site. Potential clients browse the work by keywords and, if you choose your keywords well, you'll have a better chance of connecting with clients.

□ **DesignCrowd.com**

This site is similar to 99 Designs, but with fewer active designers. This site runs contests similar to 99 Designs, but they pay out lower amounts. However, both of these facts can help if you're a new designer. First of all, there is less competition as a result of the lower pay, meaning that you stand a better chance of being selected. It's a great way to build your starting portfolio.

□ **SmashingMagazine.com**

This is a great job board with resources for both developers and designers. It's easy to find freelancing jobs, even though you have to sort through the postings yourself.

Developer Freelance Websites

These sites are for developers, though people often lump designers and developers together, you can check out both this list and the one above.

◻ **Gun.io**

If you believe you have the engineering skills to land freelance jobs with top companies like Tesla, Cisco, and Zappos, then this is the site for you. It's one of the best freelancing sites because of how they vet both companies that hire freelancers and the remote developers applying for gigs on the platform. If you get in on this site, you stand a greater chance of getting work since most freelance jobs are filled in less than 48 hours. That's a win for both the freelancer and the client.

◻ **AskLorem.com**

This site is on the rise as one of the best sites for landing short-term freelance work for designing, building, and fixing websites. It's been featured in major publications like TechCrunch, The Wall Street Journal, and CNBC. Part of the reason it's appealing to clients is because there is no monthly fee to list freelance jobs, and most gigs pay between $25 and $250. One thing to keep in mind is that the Lorem team hand-vets the freelancers they allow on the platform, which means you'll have to apply to become one of their experts. However, once you're in, you can be assured a good chance of finding consistent work.

◻ Joomlancers.com

This is the site for those who know their way around techno-logy, as this site has a fast sign up process and allows you to start bidding on jobs almost immediately. The site focuses mostly on intermediate to advanced projects, so it will not be the place for beginners.

- **BetterTeam.com**

  This is the site for freelance programmers, developers, and even designers. It's also free to sign up.

- **10XManagement.com**

  This site is good for all sorts of tech freelancers—from developers to cybersecurity experts. If you have a niche tech specialty, this is the site for you. It's also good if you just have an interest and want to see what's possible.

- **Gigster.com**

  This is also a great site for various kinds of tech workers, with jobs on the site for software designers, web designers, and even app developers. There is a screening process, so you have to pass that first; however once you're in, the site uses AI to match you with projects. This is a great site if you have some experience.

Marketer Freelance Websites

A number of the sites already mentioned also list jobs for marketers; however, these specific sites are geared more toward marketing specializations.

- **PeoplePerHour.com**

  This is a great site for both marketers and SEO experts and software engineers. And, this site takes care of pretty much everything in the process, but they will only allow you to submit 15 free applications, before paying for more. You can browse for free though, and so, you can check it out to see if the site is right for you.

- **Remotive.io**

  This is a fairly standard board with a variety of categories, including marketing. It's easy to see when a new job has been posted, where it's located, and the specialty within marketing under which it falls. What's more is that this site is completely free to use.

◻ **Aquent.com**

This company will make connections for you. The clients contact them, then they match the freelancer to the client. Their focus is mainly on marketing, but there are also a few tech and creative jobs as well.

Virtual Assistant Freelancer Websites

These include jobs like research, data entry, bookkeeping, and answering emails. Additionally, virtual assistants can specialize in a number of areas depending on their client's needs. These are some of the best sites for finding remote work:

◻ **BelaySolutions.com**

This company offers virtual assistant work for their clients, and the work is always remote. It's definitely worth checking this site out to see if they have any openings within your specialty area.

◻ **TimeEtc.com**

This site specializes in virtual assistant space, so it's great for those who are looking for this kind of work.

◻ **ClickWorker.com**

This site has various tasks like writing, data entry, and researching. You have to take a quick assessment test, but once you get access to their job board, you will find that all kinds of companies post on their site. That includes large companies like PayPal. This is a great place to get started fast in virtual assistant freelancing.

- **MTurk.com (Amazon Mechanical Turk)**

  One of the big advantages of this site is that it allows you to find quick work fast. In fact, you can begin competing for jobs within an hour of getting on the site. There are also always numerous virtual assistant jobs, though one downside is that many of them don't pay that much.

- **VAnetworking.com**

  This is a great site for networking with other virtual assistants, and it has a great job board for finding freelance work. This site also provides resources appropriate for beginners and veterans alike.

- **AssistantMatch.com**

  This is another site that makes the connections for you. They will match your skills to the right client, though the pay isn't great for the beginners. Still, they do offer training for beginners, which can make it well worth your time.

Customer Support Freelance Websites

If you're into sales but don't like working in a store or driving to work, there are freelance and remote sales jobs available. The following sites can help you find them.

- **WeWorkRemotely.com**

  This site is for freelance workers of all kinds, along with numerous customer support jobs posted.

- **VirtualVocations.com**

  This site has a huge number of remote and freelance customer support jobs.

- **SupportDriven.com**

This is one of the few dedicated customer support freelance

job boards out there. It's definitely worth your time to check it out if customer support is part of your niche of freelance work.

As you can see, there are a variety of freelance job sites you can use to find work. You can also leverage your existing network and connections from previous jobs. The point is that there are many ways you can find freelance work. The sites we went over in this chapter can give you an idea of where to find jobs quickly, and many other sites are also growing on the internet. The work is there and, if you organize your freelance business well, you can find enough work to not only survive, but thrive.

Chapter Summary

In this chapter, you've learned about the types of freelance work available along with some of the best sites where you can find that work. We specifically covered the following topics:

- Finding freelance work that pays well.
- The specific kinds of freelance jobs pay well.
- Trending freelance jobs sites for both broad and specific types of work.

In the next chapter, we will go over what to avoid with freelance work.

---

[12] https://www.cnbc.com/2019/12/14/highest-paying-freelance-jobs-of-2020-where-you-earn-90000-or-more.html

Chapter **SIX**

FREELANCE OPPORTUNITIES— WHAT TO LOOK OUT FOR

Freelance work is not without its challenges, and there are pitfalls you'll want to avoid. It's important to understand the common mistakes before you get into this type of work.

Pitfalls to Avoid

While the coronavirus crisis may have pushed you into this type of work, you may find that you enjoy it in the end because of its flexibility, freedom, and various independent career paths. Therefore, to make sure you can achieve those ideals, watch out for the following pitfalls:

1. *Thinking like an employee*—it may be hard to get past the idea of traditional work culture. When you first start working for yourself, whether it's in freelance work or as an entrepreneur, it'll be easier to keep that 9 to 5 mentality. However, one of the worst mistakes you can make is limiting your hours while

waiting for freelance jobs to come your way. You will be responsible for marketing yourself, updating your own skills, negotiating and monitoring for your services, and prioritizing projects to meet deadlines. That means working long hours frequently to keep your business running smoothly. Nevertheless, if you put in the hours, you'll soon find that you have steady work and repeat clients that will take a lot of that pressure off. You'll also find yourself getting more efficient with your skills, and you will be able to finish your jobs faster.

2. *Simply following directions*—you may be used to doing this in your traditional job, but now you are not an employee, you are a consultant, partner, and skilled expert at what you do. In some languages, a freelancer is translated as an independent expert. Your clients provide you with the rationale, background information, and parameters for the project, but it is you who brings the knowledge, expertise, and a new perspective to the job.

You need to think of yourself as equal to your client. The two of you are collaborating on the project, and you are taking the initiative. You have to take the bull by the horns and be ready to advise your client on what you know works for the project. Your opinion is part of the value you bring to the client.

Employees often feel that their company does not care much about their opinion, but the latter often does listen. Your opinion really matters and must be clearly articulated. If you are not sure, you still want to mention the possibilities to the client. If you know something is probable or that a particular result is dependent on factors that neither of you can control, you need to explain that to the client. They will appreciate your candor.

3. *Scattershot approach to finding clients and accepting every project*—it may be tempting to take any project that comes your way, particularly at first, but this is a mistake. Likewise, you also

need to systematize the way you find clients. You would start by identifying your ideal client, getting your portfolio and website together, then approaching only those clients for whom you know you can produce good work products. While the online job boards can get you started, referrals, word-of-mouth advertising, and your personal and professional networks will be the best ways to find clients.

4. *Accepting low pay*—it's easy to fall into the trap of accepting less pay for a variety of reasons. You might like the client or think you need the experience, but the reality is that you only need to accept a price that really reflects your true value. If you want to make a sustainable living, you'll need to charge what you're worth. However, if a dumping price can give you a higher chance of landing jobs with a client for your standard prices, you can use that strategy. In addition, during the coronavirus crisis, it may become difficult to find a sustainable job; therefore, you may need to reconsider your standard prices.

5. *Poor communication*—you should never take anything for the obvious. When you are working with a client, you need to have crystal clear communication, so you fully understand what they truly want. That will be to your advantage, because you don't want to produce something they are not satisfied with—that will only result in bad reviews. Communicate early, clearly, and often with your clients. Respond promptly to any questions or messages they send and make sure they know from the outset how to contact you and when you can be reached. The best practice is to document everything agreed to, along with the basis for and results of each communication. Misunderstanding happens frequently, and you can help avoid that by documenting your understanding of the communication meticulously as you go. Then, you can send notes from a meeting or after a communication detailing your interpretation of the event. Once the client confirms them, they also become bound to them.

6. *Failing to suggest another project or losing client connections—* your current or past clients are great possible future clients. So, when the current project is coming to an end, if it is appropriate to do so, suggest another possible project. If a new project isn't a current possibility at the moment, be sure to keep in contact with that client so you're the first on their mind when a new potential project comes up.

Send them emails on occasion showing that you care about them. Clients will remember those who stood with them during the coronavirus crisis. They also prefer to have a pool of proven freelancers—when they have an opportunity, it becomes convenient for them to send you an email asking whether you are available for another job.

Also, when you propose the first contract, don't include an end date. That way, the next time the client sends you an offer, it can become a contract once you accept it. The client will value you more from the first day because they will see you want to build a long-term relationship over making a quick buck.

7. *Missed deadlines—*this mistake will kill your freelance business very quickly. If you want those great reviews and word-of-mouth advertising that will bring you more clients, make sure to meet your deadlines. If, for some reason, you can't meet a deadline, be sure to communicate with the client and ensure they understand the situation. However, that should be the exception, not the rule. When you are responsible for missing the deadline, offer a price discount or an extra value to the client. They will see that you are being responsible and want to provide added value to the client. Meeting deadlines is a critical part of professional behavior and, if you miss deadlines repeatedly, your clients will go elsewhere, so take great pains to avoid this error. **91**

8. ***Getting angry with a client*—**it's true that clients can be exasperating, but you should never get angry with them. Blow off steam elsewhere, find someone to vent to, or simply walk away from the computer or telephone until you calm down. Remember the old adage: *"the customer is always right."* That applies to clients too. You need to maintain a professional attitude at all times, or you will lose clients fast. As a freelancer or an entrepreneur, keep the highest professional standards and never compromise, regardless of the client's behavior.

9. ***Putting all your eggs in one basket*—**you don't want to have just one or two clients because it is always a possibility that a client can no longer pay you for an ongoing project or you could lose a client for reasons outside your control. It is vital as a freelance worker to have multiple sources of income, and building up several months' worth of savings to get through lean time is ideal.

10. ***Taking on too many projects at once*—**this is the other side of the coin to the point above. You need more than just one or two sources of income, but taking on too many jobs will reduce the quality of your work, which may result in bad reviews. Nobody can work crazy hours for very long. You will become efficient as a freelancer, but that also means that, after 8 hours of work, you will get tired. If this situation occurs too often, you will eventually burn out. Remember that flexibility is an advantage of self-employment, so if you have too many projects at once, take a step back and work on fewer projects. Make those decisions strategically. If you have to choose between two job offers, select the one with the larger long-term benefit, which will likely be a recurring client.

Clients to Avoid

Aside from making certain mistakes as you work for clients, there are also clients that you are wise to avoid. Although you may think accepting every project that comes your way is the best way to do your business, there are some clients who will never be satisfied or will constantly make your life miserable when you work with them. To help you stay productive and enjoy your work, here is a list of clients it's best to avoid:

- **"I don't know what I want"**

  If the client doesn't really know what they want, you will both end up frustrated. Before you accept a client, you should discuss their goals in detail so you can make sure they have a clear idea of what they hope to accomplish. Their goals should also be specific. For example, merely saying, "I want to increase web traffic," is not specific enough. What does that mean? By how much? In what time frame? Once you have a better understanding of what the client wants to achieve, make sure you can deliver it. If the scope is something you can't guarantee or deliver on, be honest and tell the client you may not be right for what they want to do. Trying to take on something you can't deliver will only result in frustration and bad reviews.

  On the other hand, your client may not be an expert on web traffic, thus wants to hire you. In this case, it would be your responsibility—and a great opportunity—to offer one or more solutions. If the client is not willing to agree on specific conditions, do not enter such a relationship because both sides will be disappointed.

- **Houdini**

  This is the type of client who doesn't answer their emails or phone, and sometimes completely disappears altogether. It can delay your progress and cause big problems when you need to make important transactions, like getting paid. With such clients, whenever you need a quick answer to a question, it can become frustrating if your work is held up while you wait to get that answer.

This kind of client is hard to identify from the start, but if you start seeing this pattern within your first few interactions, you may need to let the client know that their behavior is not something you can work with. It's worth cutting them loose if they don't plan to work with you to produce good, timely work. If you received the client through a freelance web page, your fee for the milestone should be secured. However, if you have a direct contract with the client, make sure there are clauses ensuring you will get paid for a milestone, even if you could not finish it due the client's lack of availability.

□ **The Barterer**

Exchanging services has its place in the freelance world; for example, it can be a great way to partner with a new client. However, you have to be sure everyone involved is benefiting from the deal. Clients who want to exchange services or products you don't need or want aren't really offering you something of value, so don't make those deals. Since you can't barter to pay your bills, this should be the exception rather than the rule.

□ **Mr. or Ms. Wrong**

This client has gone through many freelancers and, just like a bad boy or party girl, there's probably a good reason for it. You might think you can change the client or that you'll finally be the one to satisfy them, but the reality is, if so many others have failed before you, it's unlikely you'll be the one to make this client happy. In addition, doing lots of work for a client who will never be happy will be unlikely to land you a good review.

Thus, before you agree to work with a client, learn a bit about their past experience with other professionals. Ask them about other freelancers they've worked with, what made them look for someone else, and consider whether those past freelancers are people you know who have good track records. If they do, the problem may be with the client and not with the freelancers. Some freelancing platforms like Upwork show reviews the client gave on the freelancer and vice versa. If any side has three stars or less, read those comments carefully and be warned if the client's average score is below 4 stars.

One of the most important things to remember as a freelance worker is that you have valuable services to offer clients, so don't sell yourself short. Don't accept every job that comes your way, avoid accepting clients who are never satisfied or are micromanagers, and charge appropriately for your services. The services you are offering are valuable, and you are partnering with your clients—you are *not* their employee. Basically, when you make the switch to freelance work, you have to adjust your mindset to recognize that you are a general manager of your freelance business now. You will serve your client as an equal by providing valuable services or products. Once you adjust your thinking, you can then achieve a successful, fulfilling life in the gig economy.

Chapter Summary

In this chapter, we've looked at some of the more common pitfalls you can make as a freelance worker, and we've also discussed certain types of clients you should avoid. Specifically, we covered the following topics:

- Common freelance mistakes.
- Changing your mindset.
- Professional behavior.
- Communication.
- You are an equal to the client and will provide professional services.

In the next chapter, we will cover the various forms of online and remote entrepreneurial opportunities.

Chapter SEVEN

ONLINE ENTREPRENEURSHIP OPPORTUNITIES

IN this chapter, we will be going over the best online business and entrepreneurial opportunities you can partake in. It's helpful first to understand the difference between online entrepreneurship and business opportunities compared to freelancing work. While it is advisable to set up any freelance work you do as a business, there is a difference between working as a freelancer and starting your own online business.

With the former, you have clients telling you their requirements. That differs from starting your own business, in that you will be offering specific, pre-identified services or products to customers. That means you will have to define customer needs and determine how you can meet those needs. This is something that may entail an initial financial investment, and it will most certainly require a time investment to get set up.

Another difference is in the risk and opportunities associated with freelancing versus owning your own business. Freelancers don't really risk losing their businesses and they don't have to make any big investment that they have to worry about losing either. On the other hand, their earnings are limited by their hourly price and the time they can work. Business owners can lose all their investments and even the entire business, but have no upper limit on how much they can earn. As long as their product or service is in demand, they can become millionaires.

The higher limit with businesses can be an exciting thought. It is also one of the better ways to achieve a dream of financial freedom, better lifestyle for you and your family, and the opportunity to do something you really enjoy. So, how would you get started? The great thing about an online business is that all you need to get started is a phone, computer, and internet connection; the hard part is coming up with a good business idea. Such involves the consideration of at least the three following things:

1. You want it to be something you enjoy doing.

2. You want it to be something you do well.

3. It needs to be in demand; in other words, it should be something people will pay for. This last point is the most important consideration you should take. If you have identified a high demand for something you don't enjoy or aren't good at producing, then you can hire freelancers who will do that job for you. It will be more expensive and maybe not as enjoyable as some other jobs, but you can still earn a lot with a good business idea.

To help you decide on the business that will work best for you, we will be looking at some of the best options in this category. These will include easy startup business ideas, along with more profitable and in-demand options.

Great Online Business Ideas

The following business opportunities are categorized according to their general business type. Many of these businesses overlap with freelancing, and freelancing can be a stepping stone to starting your own online business. As a freelance worker, you learn to navigate a number of personal risks, make important decisions, and advertise your services. These skills all prepare you for business ownership, thus if you don't think you're ready to be an entrepreneur yet, you can start with freelancing. The main difference between freelancing and owning your own business is that, as a business owner, you would decide which activities you want to perform yourself and which to outsource. Therefore, have an open mind—it is normal to outsource accounting and tax matters to a professional, so don't be afraid to delegate other tasks as needed. You merely cannot delegate the ultimate responsibility for the business, which is no different from what any other CEO would do.

You are the CEO or managing director of your business. You may be your sole employee in some cases, but you can outsource work as appropriate when you are the business owner. The CEO in a large company wouldn't do the work associated with production; rather, they would make decisions and ensure the necessary work is all completed. In a small or one-person company, the CEO may have to do certain work; however, their main responsibility is to make good business decisions. The CEO should outsource all activities unless they can do them very well. The CEO must also take responsibility for any poor decisions made within and around their business. We all make mistakes, but the CEO must be mature enough to learn from their own mistakes.

A number of online businesses may seem like freelance jobs—though they may be providing freelance services, there are various important differences between a business that use freelance labor and selling services. Though a business may start out as an individual who was both doing work in and running the business, that would often change quickly as the business grows. Many businesses that provide online services use several freelance workers to provide their clients with high quality services. They connect the client with the freelancer, then pay the freelancer once the product or service is completed. Thus, with these online business opportunities, though you may start out small with just yourself working, the focus would be to grow your business to where you would be outsourcing the lion's share of the work you're doing for your clients.

Publishing Businesses

If you're running a publishing business, then you're producing content. That can be done for direct sales profits, such as with publishing and selling a book, or indirectly by producing a blog ultimately designed to generate, for example, an email list of potential customers.

- *Blogging services*—right now, it's easier than ever before to start a blog. If you know what you're doing, it can be a great source of income. The key is to monetize it, which you can do in a few ways. If you are selling a product or service on a website, your blog can help to generate an email list when offering your products or services. You can even outsource the blog writing to qualified freelancers. Another way to earn money with a blog is to combine it with affiliate marketing— you may go check out the description of that under "Marketing Businesses," below, but this is essentially when you market someone else's products or services and earn a commission on the sales.

  If you're diligent in your efforts, blogging can become quite profitable—in some cases, bloggers can make more than **101**

$50,000 per year. There are several sites where you can create a blog for a minimal investment, and many of these blog sites will provide you with the tools to help increase the traffic to your site, including keyword identifiers to help your site rank higher in the search engines. However, as the business owner, it's also possible to outsource the site management to freelancers.

Blogging by itself is often done for free and does not generate large income, though it's still really a great way to get an online business started. If you can successfully attract people to your site, those same people may become your future customers. There is, however, another way to do business in blogging—you can create a business that provides blogs to clients for publication on their websites. With this model, you would contract out blog-writing services by pairing a blogger with the client. Again, if you're just starting out, that could mean you're initially writing blogs for several clients, but you can start hiring other freelancers to write the blogs under your name as your business grows.

- *Self-publish a book on Amazon*—no matter if you're looking to write the Great American Novel or pay a freelancer to write it, Amazon makes publishing easy. There are a number of guides out there that can help you to both write the book and have it actually generate income. In fact, platforms like Amazon provide writers and publishers with tools that allow them to search a topic of interest and view the selling success of other books in that category.

There are two ways you can go with a self-published book: the first is fiction books that people enjoy reading, whereas the second is nonfiction books that people read to learn about specific topics. Both can be lucrative, but it's important that they are written to appeal to their respective audiences, as well as marketed appropriately. You can, once again, outsource the writing to a freelance writer, and you can also outsource the marketing task. As the business owner, you will need to oversee that each part of the process is done in accordance with your business model. If you're thinking of going this route, it's also advisable to continue and publish several books while they are mutually supporting sales. They don't have to be long, and if you market them correctly, they can bring in significant amounts of money each month.

Marketing is the key to generating high sales of your books. It's a great idea to run a promotion in the first week and advertise to your email list and across all your social media platforms to generate higher sales. If you can generate high enough sales in the first week on a platform like Amazon, they will then start to help you promote the book, which is how to start really making money as a writer or self-publisher.

◻ *Copywriting*—This is both the art and science of getting people to take action on a cause, and can be either written or spoken. Copywriters can write sales pages, emails, and blog content. It's also a lucrative field if you become good enough at it. As a business owner, you can supply copywriting services to a number of potential clients—that is, anyone who advertises—and you can outsource the writing, so you can concentrate on attracting clients and finding highly talented freelancers to write for them.

◻ *Technical writing*—Technical writing is a solid field in which to start a business. It is projected to grow faster than average at approximately 8% between now and 2028[13] (U.S. Bureau of Labor Statistics, 2019), making it a great business opportunity. Technical writers write instruction manuals for things like your TV, building a coffee stand, how your car operates, among other jobs. If you start a business in this area, you will likely be able to find numerous clients with writing you can again outsource to qualified freelancers.

103

- *Resume and cover letter writing*—this field can generate more than $1000 per month in income. You would structure the service in accordance with the types of clients and their needs. An entry-level resume would be at the lower end at around $400, but an executive resume or that which is specific to a particular field would cost much more. Customers would also be willing to pay more for a quick turnaround[14] (Truex, 2018). If you can attract the clients to your business, you can maintain a stable of writers who can generate solo resumes and resume packages containing cover letters and, often, follow-up letters.

Marketing Businesses

These are businesses in which you would help someone sell their products or services. Depending on the type of marketing you offer, you could earn either a commission on the sales or a fee for creating effective ads.

- *Affiliate marketing*—this involves promoting someone else's product and earning a commission as you do so. There are a few ways you can follow through with this service, the first being promoting products like ebooks, memberships, video series, among other informational products. The provision ranges between 5% and 50% percent, or it is a fixed amount. It has low barriers to entry, and it's easy to find products to promote.

Another way to do this is to partner with an affiliate program. Amazon, Commission Junction, and Clickbank are three such programs you can consider. They offer easy entrances into affiliate marketing, and you can affiliate quickly with numerous well-known companies that pay good commissions. There are millions of profitable products to choose from too. It is helpful to have some knowledge of SEO and copywriting if you want to get into affiliate marketing; however, as a business owner, you can still outsource these skills while you work on finding clients and sales channels.

◻ *SEO*—SEO stands for Search Engine Optimization, which refers to getting websites or blog posts to rank higher in search engines such as Google. The key is understanding the search terms that people use when looking for products, services, or information. The higher a website ranks, the more traffic it receives and revenue the owner makes. This is a highly-valued skill in internet marketing, but it can be challenging since search engines like Google frequently change their algorithms, along with some of the rules. Therefore, if your business specializes in SEO services, you will need to make sure you're always up-to-date on the newest strategies.

◻ *Facebook advertising*—as Facebook continues to grow, businesses are beginning to spend more on Facebook advertisements, but many of them don't actually understand Facebook ads. That will be where your business comes in. If you are, can become, or hire a Facebook ad specialist, you can offer to create effective Facebook ads for them as a service. If you don't know how to do it yourself, it's something you can learn fairly quickly, or you can outsource that work as the business owner. Like any advertising service, the potential for a business to earn a good income is quite high when you assist clients in driving their measurable outcomes, save them time, and provide them with proven expertise.

◻ *Lead generation*—leads are the lifeblood of businesses. Lead generation is the process of attracting and converting prospective customers into individuals interested in a business' product or service. Businesses are always looking to generate new leads, and, if you create a business that can assist with that, you can then make a good income. This is probably the single most important aspect of a business; therefore, if you can connect your clients with a good lead generator, they will pay well for that service. **105**

Sales Companies

There are a number of different ways you can engage in online sales. These business opportunities can help you earn a good income with little overhead or initial investment.

- *Set up an e-commerce site*—for many e-commerce markets, you're competing against old school business people who may not have much experience in online marketing. That can give you a distinct advantage, but it does require some hard work. The first stepping stone would be that you have to stand out among hundreds of thousands of other e-commerce websites. However, if you can find the right niche and execute the appropriate marketing techniques, you can have success with your e-commerce store.

   To do that, you'll want to brainstorm ideas for a profitable market, and some strategic keyword research will help you here. The next thing to consider is whether the product is a high or low margin product. Low margin products would require a high turnover to generate good profit. The margin is the difference between the selling price and purchase price, and it must cover all your expenses and generate a certain profit. Finally, you will want to ensure the product is something within a growth market. If it's already passed its peak, you should look at something else, preferably an industry on the upswing.

   Once you have the product, you'll need to create a good-looking store quickly. This can be done with a minimal investment, and you don't have to be a coder to do it. Shopify is one such user-friendly site, and its 30-day free trial won't have you spending a dime to get started.

- *Sell products on eBay*—this may be considered old-school now, but you can still make lots of money selling on its platform. You can start by buying something simple, like clothing on sale, then list it on eBay for a higher price. If it sells, you can then reinvest the profit by buying more items to continue making more profit. It requires a bit of strategy, but it can still be a profitable online business.

◻ *Buy and flip domains*—this is similar to those realtors who buy and flip real estate, except you're doing it in the virtual world. Just like with realtors, you would buy domains—perhaps fixing them up a bit—then sell them for a profit. It can generate pretty good money, particularly if you try to get ahead of trends and purchase hot item domains.

Information for Sale

With these kinds of online businesses, you would basically be monetizing your expertise. There are a couple of ways you can do that.

◻ *Create online courses*—there are a few different platforms where you can do this. Udemy.com is a site where you can create the course and earn a percentage of the profits. You can also earn a greater percentage for students who find your course through your own advertising. You don't have to have a PhD to offer a course—you can create a course on, for example, how to change the oil in your car or how to paint a mountain landscape, all without formal education on the topic. Anything you have expertise on can be the subject matter for one of these courses. You can also self-publish a text to go along with your course to create two sources of income, while marketing each.

◻ *Coaching*—coaching is a hot, new trend these days, and there also exist several kinds of coaches, including life coaches, health coaches, dating coaches, among others. For this kind of business, you would need expertise in some topic, along with video conferencing capabilities through platforms like Skype, Zoom, or Google Hangouts. Essentially, you and your client **107** would be calling daily, weekly, or monthly depending on the preference, and you would help them with the topic of coaching you offer. It's also helpful for marketing if you have a blog on your coaching topic or publish an ebook to generate another income stream.

- *Start a podcast*—podcasts are great revenue generators. Once again, if you have expertise in some area, you can start a podcast in which you discuss the topic, invite guests for interviews, and take questions from listeners. As you grow your podcast, you can then begin to offer paid sponsorships and/or sell your own products and services. By earning the trust of your listeners, they will become much more likely to buy what you're selling.

- *Become a YouTuber*—YouTube videos are all the rage these days, so if you like being in front of the camera, you can speak directly to your audience and build a lucrative online business. Among topics to choose from, you could pitch products, voice your opinions, educate people, react to games or other videos, and much more. Your revenue comes from advertising in your videos and affiliated sales. Along with that, and with no more than just your smartphone, you can produce and upload videos starting today, though many YouTubers will tell you it's worth the investment to have a good microphone and stage setup.

Design and Development Businesses

If you're a technology nerd, these businesses can be a way to make considerable profits. There are a number of different opportunities available in this niche.

- *App development*—mobile apps continue to be as popular as ever, and this could be a lucrative option if you have a cool idea for a fun or useful app. It's helpful to have coding knowledge for this option; however, if you don't, you can still probably find someone who does who would be willing to collaborate on creating your app. Because there are so many apps out there right now, you'll want to validate your idea first before you invest any time or money in it.

- *Web developer*—this is someone who can build a website from the bottom up. You'll definitely need to choose a development framework suitable for the type and features of web pages you want to create. It can take time to learn, but it's worth the effort because this niche pays well and the demand is continuously growing.

- *Graphic design*—graphic designers are visual communicators. They design web pages, sale pages, logos, and any other polished and professional graphics. When you see a web page that is well-organized and easy to use, that's thanks to a graphic designer. To be good at this job, you don't necessarily have to be able to draw, have a college degree, or even have a fancy computer. You do, however, need to be someone who thinks visually, and you'll need to specialize in a specific form of design or topic. You will be creating a good user experience with graphical user interface features.

- *Build niche sites*—niche sites target a specific audience. For example, a niche site would not just be a site about photography, but it would also be a site about landscape photography. By targeting that specific niche, you would likely receive a higher rank on Google for keyword searches, then, of course, you would want to turn that traffic into earnings. That can be done by either selling your own products or through affiliate marketing. This type of business has a really high workload; however, if you can create a good niche site, it can bring in an extra $500 in monthly earnings or more.

Other Online Businesses

The following are several potentially lucrative online businesses.

◻ *Consulting*—if you have specific knowledge that is helpful to other businesses, you can get paid as a consulting firm for them. You'll have to be able to apply the knowledge, skills, and experience you have to help solve problems for their company. Compared to freelance consultancy, you can hire a team or use professional freelancers to offer complex services and scale the business.

◻ *Instagram sponsorships*—if taking photos and building a huge following on Instagram is your dream, you can find some sponsorship opportunities that will pay you to do just that. If, for example, your account is about all things fitness, you could sponsor products like supplements or gym equipment, which could then make you a lot of money if you're a social media influencer.

◻ *Tech support*—here, you would be offering your skills as a tech whiz, which is a valuable skill in this day and age. You can work with big companies or one-on-one with clients. Either way, you will likely gain lots of business in this field.

◻ *Accounting, processing documents, and administrative services*—the focus of these firms would be to prepare financial documents, provide bookkeeping services, provide document processing services, and offer a variety of administrative services to any number of clients.

This list of options is by no means exhaustive, but they are areas where you can get your remote business set up and start making money relatively quickly. These are business opportunities that will not only allow you to survive the coronavirus crisis, but also realize your dreams of a major lifestyle change fully.

You can make money in a way that also gives you the freedom

to live life on your own terms. You can also love what you do and have plenty of time for family, friends, and fun. Next, I will be taking you through how to get set up in an online entrepreneurial business.

Chapter Summary

In this chapter, we've gone over various entrepreneurial opportunities available online. Specifically, I've covered the following topics:

- Difference between an online business and online freelancing.
- Discovering the type of online business you'd like to create.
- Different categories of online businesses.
- Specific kinds of online businesses you can create quickly with minimal cash investment.

In the next chapter, we'll be going over how to start up your online business.

[13] https://www.bls.gov/ooh/media-and-communication/technical-writers.htm

[14] https://www.thebalancesmb.com/how-to-start-a-resume-writing-service-3957645

Chapter **EIGHT**

ONLINE ENTREPRENEURSHIP– GETTING SET UP

WHILE it might seem daunting to start a business, starting up an online business is actually much easier than you may think, despite it requiring some forethought. It also requires a fundamental change in mindset. Before I talk about that, however, let me give you a definition for an online business. Essentially, an online business requires that you market and advertise it, attract customers, process payments, deliver products, and manage all the other components online for the most part.

Another important factor for any business owner to consider—not just those online—is that you have to change your mindset. As I discussed with making the change from employee to freelancer, there is another fundamental shift when making the leap to the business owner. If you're creating your own business, you have to identify your customers and their needs, then create products or services that address those needs. You also need to be able to deliver in a way that gives them the most value for their money. You are no longer simply an employee or even a self-employed freelancer being directed by

114

a boss or client; you are now the business owner. Therefore, you—and only you—are responsible for your own success or failure. It's important that you think about it from that perspective. With this in mind, let's look at how you can get your new business up and running.

Step #1: Research

The first thing you need to do is research the market for your specific niche. Make sure you learn what works and what doesn't so you don't make the same mistakes others have made. You need to look into how you can monetize your ideas and passions. Will your decided business work? Is there a market for it? What does it take to monetize it? You will want to learn as much as you can about your idea to give your business the best chance for success.

Step #2: Identifying Your Audience and Your Competition

You need to know who your clients are and identify how you plan to help them. You need to ask yourself the following questions:

1. What customers' problem does my business solve?

2. Who needs my service?

3. Why should they pick my business over the competition?

One way to figure out if people will be interested in what you are offering is to use a keyword tool and see how frequently people search for your service. Google's keyword tool will return information on the number of searches conducted each month worldwide. Thus, it's a good idea to direct your attention toward niches with between 10,000 and 50,000 searches each month. The keyword tool also lets you know if the competition in that market is high, medium, or low, and you can also insert your keywords in a Google search and see how many results are returned. Researching keywords will give you a great idea of the level of competition.

Step #3: Write a Business Plan

It is imperative that you have a plan and stick to it as much as possible. With a business plan, you'll want to, once again, identify the problem your business solves, your target market, and how you can reach them. Furthermore, you'll want to identify your startup costs, so you know the costs for getting the business up and running.

You'll also want to determine your pricing models and business expenses. If you plan to outsource work, you'll want to identify how you will find those freelancers and figure out a price range for their services, which should be included in your business expenses. With your expenses identified, you can then determine the amount you'll be charging for your services or product.

Make sure you also identify the risks, obstacles, and competition you will be encountering, along with your strategies for overcoming all these problems. At the very end, describe what success looks like. This last part of your business plan is critical, as it helps keep you focused and motivated. Changes will be necessary to the overall plan in some cases; however, you should document them to keep track.

Step #4: Name, Domain, and Website

Just as you did with the freelance business entity, you will want to choose a name, purchase a domain—which is not very expensive—and set up a website. At this stage, you will need to create your business entity. If you're setting up your business in the United States, the same business structures discussed earlier apply; although, for starting a business, an LLC or C-Corps will be your best options, particularly because you will be outsourcing work. Those entities will give your company the best potential for growth. There are different models in other countries, and you'll want to investigate the options in your area if you're located outside the US.

You also need to have a website where you can direct potential clients, build email lists, post blogs, and offer your services. For that, it will be best to have a domain name that's easy to remember, which will make it easier for people to find it. Your website will be essential to your business' success and, for that reason, it may be worth hiring a website designer. You will want to get started on the right foot, so it's best to make sure everything is as perfect as it can possibly be before you launch your business. Hiring a website designer can help ensure your online presence is attractive and client-friendly, giving prospective clients a good first impression.

Step #5: Finances

If you need startup money, make sure you save enough to cover your expenses and provide a cushion until you can begin to make a profit. You will also want to make sure you have a bank account set up to handle your money as it comes in and need to pay for expenses.

Step #6: Sign Up for an Email Delivery Service

As long as it's stood, email is still the most productive way to promote and market your business online. These services take care of sending emails to your clients and prospective clients. One example of this kind of service is MailChimp, which is a leader in the market. Your account on their service is free, which is a great place to start. They also have an exceptionally user-friendly website and provide training videos to help you make sure your business is a success.

Step #7: Marketing Your Business

Building a website isn't enough—you have to attract traffic to your website. There are two main ways you can do this: the free way and the paid way. The free way involves a greater time investment before seeing results, whereas the paid way accelerates the income. The free way would include generating email lists and making use of your social media platforms, which can work, even if it does take more time.

If you want quicker results, you will want to advertise your business online, which can bring you traffic instantly. There are a number of different ways you can do this—one that is often a great place to start is Google AdWords. It can get you great results, though you do need to understand how to use it, or you will end up generating more losses than wins. Your page will rank at the top of Google searches, and you would pay for every click that directs users to your page. It might also be worthwhile to outsource that to a marketing pro. If you can afford to do that, you should receive strong and fast results.

Step #8: Network

Even though you're taking your business online, it doesn't necessarily mean that you would stop being part of your professional community. You can join a forum within your niche, for example, and that can be a great source of information and inspiration. You can comment on blogs within your niche, engage in Twitter conversations, join a Facebook or LinkedIn group, or even make professional friends on StumbleUpon or YouTube. This kind of networking gets you out there and makes other professionals aware of your presence, which can bring in referrals and ideas for making your business even better.

Step #9: Plan Your Launch

When you launch your new business, you will want to make as big a splash as you can. Thus, it's a great idea to plan promotions, such as a special pricing for the first 100 visitors to your site or during the first week of business. Promotions can generate a lot of traffic that will hopefully include return customers. Treat the initial discounts as an investment that can turn many visitors into paying customers. State it clearly that the discount is for a limited time only. Announce your launch date and time, along with any promotions anywhere you can think of—social media platforms, chatrooms, group forums, and, of course, on your company's website. Try to get the word out to as many people as possible. The bigger a splash you make in the beginning, the more traffic you can generate for those email lists.

Step #10: Don't Stop Growing and Improving

Just because you've launched your business or even achieved a few of your goals, it doesn't mean there's time to rest on your laurels. It's a never-ending journey where you are constantly learning new ways to improve your skills and grow your business; running and maintaining takes persistence and commitment. If you're not growing, then your business is dying, so don't stop learning new ways to market and promote it. You want to track everything, optimize your website, and get more conversions. A *conversion* is when you get a potential client to take an action you want, like signing up for email updates or clicking on a button to add your product to their cart. To be truly successful, you have to keep the game going. That will be how you build the business and lifestyle you've always dreamed about.

By following these ten steps, you can quickly get your online business up and running. It's relatively easy to do, and it can be done with no initial investment other than your time, though the road is easier if you have some money to invest. Once you've gotten your business up and running, you will be well on your way to that rewarding life in which you control your destiny.

Chapter Summary

In this chapter, we've gone through the main steps to take for setting up your online business. Specifically, we have covered the following topics:

- Researching your niche.
- Identifying your clients, competition, and startup needs.
- Getting your business entity created and setting up your on-line presence.
- Finding clients, marketing, and drawing traffic to your website.
- Planning your launch, networking, and maintaining growth.

In the next chapter, we will cover the most realistic online businesses and go over examples of successful online models.

Chapter **NINE**

ONLINE ENTREPRENEURIAL EXAMPLES AND SITES

There are lots of great online business opportunities, and the reality is that you can launch and make good money with an online business for very little or even no capital investment. If you understand how online marketing works, or you're a whiz at social media, you'll likely find setting up and running an online business pretty easy. So, what kinds of businesses are the most likely to make good money right now?

Entrepreneurial Winners

There are a number of business opportunities that are trending now. Let's take a look at why they work and why they're likely to continue being winning models.

◻ **Chatbot Business**

With the popularity of Facebook and other social media platforms, people have grown accustomed to chatting with friends and family, even if they're located on the other side of the world. That is precisely why chatbots powered by artificial intelligence (AI) present a great opportunity for entrepreneurs looking to help businesses automate and reduce the manpower it takes to chat with customers.

Businesses across all spectrums are taking advantage of this kind of technology. Numerous platforms—such as Manychat and ChattyPeople—are cropping up and taking the complexity out of building a chatbot. In fact, there is now a stampede of people wanting to launch chatbots to automate at least some of their sales and marketing efforts. In addition, while chatbots may help make businesses more efficient, there's also an opportunity for you to get rich selling these businesses the tools to do just that.

◻ **Subscription Box Business**

This is one business that was developed years ago, but has seen a revival in the age of the internet. Subscription boxes are a marketing strategy that involves the recurring delivery of niche products. They target a wide range of customers, even though they cater to very specific needs.

The subscription box business starts with a basic level of items the customer orders on a recurring basis. When the customer places an order, they are directed into a sales funnel that includes numerous upsells called add-ons. It's an effective strategy, and the subscription box industry saw a roughly 30 times increase between 2013 and 2016[15] (Adams 2019). The typical visitor to a subscription box site is in their early 40s. This model will work for many years of recurring sales that can make you more than $75,000 per year.

123

◻ Ad Management Business

Now, more than ever, it's all about the advertising. There's a lot of competition for customers on the internet, and you can sell your services to businesses that are hungry for people like you if you have a strong understanding of how to drive paid traffic and optimize conversions. Knowing the specifics of marketing, redirecting and improving conversions, and the ebb and flow of sales funnels can make your business a hot commodity.

Consider the fact that digital ad spending in the US is expected to surpass two-thirds of total media spending by 2023, and it is already exceeding traditional advertising[16] (eMarketer, 2019). That represents an explosive growth of online ads, and the internet is really still in its infancy. If you can capitalize on this industry, you can build a formidable online business.

◻ SEO Business

Search engine optimization is another growing business that relates to marketing. Paid ads are growing at an astounding rate, but if a business can rank higher in search engines like Google, they will be more competitive and lucrative.

Roughly 40% of people click on the first search results that pop up in their browser, and the first page accounts for 91% of the search share (Adams, 2019). Because of that, businesses will pay good money to someone who can help rank their business higher in search engine results. If your business can provide that service, you can easily capitalize on this industry.

◻ Webinar Business

Webinars are one of the better ways to sell online. The audience is already engaged in the product, thus they are ready and willing to purchase what you're offering. The best part is that you don't have to be selling your own product for you to make a fortune in this industry.

The best way to get started is to find a product that you truly believe in, then build an excellent webinar to promote it. There are even software programs that can help you build an entire webinar, including copy for ads and swipes. If you're good at it, you can build a lucrative business as a sales affiliate.

◻ **Business Coaching**

If you have a good understanding of the forces that drive purchases, you can make a great income as a business coach. There is a growing number of business coaches hired by entrepreneurs and business owners to help them find their way in the world of commerce in general, and this is now a growing field for online businesses.

The key to this field is to offer an incredible value to your clients upfront, then they will pay you for the execution of those ideas. You want to analyze your client's business to understand where it is at the moment and where they hope to take it in the future. Once you know that, you can help them devise how to get where they want to go. To be really successful in this industry, you will need some proof that you're good. Focus on getting a few customers and helping them succeed; then, you can use their testimonials to justify charging better rates.

◻ **Online Learning**

This is one area where the opportunity is growing, given the current pandemic. Online learning portals are still evolving, and a growing number of students don't want to study in conventional ways. Thus, the modern mobile lifestyle is a perfect fit for online learning platforms. You don't need to develop a university platform, though that is an option. You can, however, **125** develop online vocational learning platforms or other sub-niches like continuing education for professionals or online business training programs. Either direction will build your revenue.

◻ Online Grocery and Foods

This is another opportunity that has been highlighted in the current pandemic. It's also been growing in popularity among busy people who don't have time to go grocery shopping. In fact, busy people are target clients for this growing industry. If you have a talent for driving customers to your business and can maintain good relations with vendors, this can be a successful business for you. You can start out small and increase your services and products as your business grows.

◻ Baby Rompers Online Store Business

This is a great online business idea, particularly for stay-at-home parents. Baby rompers are dresses for babies, and nearly everyone has fallen in love with them by this point. They show a substantial search volume, and you could use baby rompers as a trending product if you want to open an online store. In addition, you can add a variety of baby clothes to help your store become a one-stop-shop for busy parents. Helping parents reduce their load can mean a big boon for your business, and you won't need a lot of experience to get started.

◻ Online Customer Engagement Platform

Customer service is one area that is vital to any business, and they are always looking for ways to attract more users. If you are someone who is skillful at communicating with people, understanding their perspective, and relaying that to a client, then this could be a great business idea for you. You would help clients engage with their customers to understand their needs better, which helps both your client and their customer get what they want. If you're good at it, this can be a great business opportunity.

◻ **Children Products**

Schools have been closed during the pandemic and children stayed at home. Their parents had to quickly discover how to entertain and educate them. Children's books and online education recorded an enormous boom and many became bestsellers overnight, literally. After the restrictions are lifted and life returns to "normal" these sales will drop. However, if the restrictions last longer, people get used to them and may find that these forms of education and entertainment have a better influence on children than TV or the internet, and may keep higher demand for these products. I mentioned just two children's products but there are many more if you look around with open eyes. Just remember that children are not your target customers, but their parents are. When you choose your products, design them to their parents' needs, what they think is good for their children.

These ideas are some of the more promising online business ideas, but there are other ways to profit from online businesses. For example, it is also possible to buy an existing, developed-online business if you have the appropriate funds. In this scenario, you would then continue building customer share and business profits.

You can buy or build a business and sell it in the future. Sales price is estimated from future years' profits. It's even possible to earn much more if you are approached by a company looking to build a dominant share of that particular market. In a sense, it's like those realtors who buy a house, fix it up, and then sell it for a profit. There are other ideas similar to this one too, and it some-times pays to think outside the box.

Whatever kind of online business you may choose, the key to succeed is to focus on customer needs and find innovative and efficient ways to serve those needs. If you can do that, you can build an enduring online business that will enable you to live your dreams. There are a few pitfalls to avoid, which will be addressed in the next chapter.

Chapter Summary

In this chapter, we went through numerous examples of promising online business opportunities in the current climate. Specifically, we covered the following topics:

- Entrepreneurial winners.
- Online businesses that involve innovative technology.
- Online businesses that involve marketing strategies.
- Entrepreneurial online business ideas.
- Business build-up, renovation, and resale.

In the next chapter, we'll go over the pitfalls to avoid with online entrepreneurship.

---

[15] https://www.entrepreneur.com/article/299734

[16] https://www.emarketer.com/newsroom/index.php/us-digital-ad-spending-will-surpass-traditional-in-2019/

Chapter TEN

ONLINE ENTREPRENEURSHIP– WHAT TO LOOK OUT FOR

IF you plan to take the leap into the online business world, you will want to do everything you can to ensure it will be successful. The internet has incredible potential, and you have an opportunity right now to jump into this profitable realm. Research shows that approximately 70% of Americans shop online, and the US e-commerce revenue in 2019 was more than $600 billion[17] (Digital Commerce 360, 2020). However, online business opportunities come with their own set of unique challenges, and you could encounter some devastating pitfalls if you don't know what to watch out for. Let's take a look at the pitfalls you'll want to avoid.

Taking Too Long to Launch

As the saying goes, timing is everything, and nowhere is that more true than when you go to launch a business. If you spend too much time researching your business or waiting for the perfect execution, you can miss your launch window. Don't let what's perfect be the enemy of the good. If you do, it's possible a competitor will beat you to the punch. Additionally, you shouldn't let yourself fall into the trap of analysis paralysis—avoid overthinking and worrying too much about being perfect. Make it good and get it out there.

Starting a Business You're Not Passionate About

If you want to start your own business, there's one thing for certain—you will spend a lot of time thinking about it and a lot of time working on it, so you'd better like it. You will have to be dedicated to sticking with it, even when the profits aren't that high. In fact, that will be when you have to stay the most invested. There will be many obstacles you might face; things like more competition than you had anticipated, and, if you aren't enthusiastic about getting up every day to make this business work, it won't. It's that simple. Your lack of enthusiasm will show in every aspect of your business, and your customers and employees will all be able to pick up on it. Therefore, whatever business you choose to start, make sure you're passionate about it.

Underestimating the Time It Will Take to Make Profit

Many businesses won't make a profit in their first year, and you have to be realistic about the work it will take to make the profit you're hoping for. You have to put in as much work for an online business as you would a brick and mortar business. It takes a lot of time, energy, and planning, and you shouldn't make the mistake of thinking it will be quick and easy. You can start to earn money relatively quickly, but that is not the same thing as making a profit. Set realistic goals and manage your expectations. You'll get there, but it will take some time.

Failing to Prepare

While it can be fast and relatively easy to start an online business, you would still have to prepare. That means doing your homework by researching your niche, identifying your clients, choosing a business model, setting your prices, preparing your marketing strategy, and personally defining success. There are many aspects of your business that will evolve over time; however, if you don't start out with a plan, you will likely never see your launch date, let alone succeed.

Fixing Something That Isn't Broken

A common reason many online businesses fail is that they are offering a product or service that doesn't solve any significant problem for their clients. Remember that a problem you identify also has to be a problem that your potential customers have identified. If they don't think it's a problem, they won't buy your solution. In addition, if you see that has happened and don't pivot your online business in a different direction, you can lose it altogether. Make sure your goal is always to address the customers' needs. If you don't do that, you won't have customers.

Dismissing Negative Feedback

It can be easy—and certainly more gratifying—to listen to your fans and ignore your critics, but this is a mistake that will completely undermine your business. You need to listen to the negative reviews, so you can understand your customers better, tweak your product as necessary, and develop top-notch customer service. Consumers will also be paying quite a bit of attention to those negative reviews, so you need to as well. Let the negative feedback guide you to improve your business, and solicit feedback regularly to keep track of customer satisfaction.

Not Being Unique Enough

You have to find a way to distinguish yourself from the competition. If too many businesses are doing the same thing, then there are too many businesses in that niche. To really get traction in your area, you have to be different and offer something that the other guy isn't. It could be a unique product, but it could also be a unique delivery method, faster delivery, or perks that others aren't offering. Ask yourself: what can I offer that my competitors can't, or how can I be different in your niche? You have to make it clear to your target audience why they should choose you over the competition.

Failing to Define Your Target Audience

You must identify who your ideal customers are and tailor your marketing efforts toward them. Understand that you simply will be unable to fill the needs of every consumer, and the object is to figure out who can use your online business best and how you can meet their needs. That will allow you to market directly to your ideal customers, generating the highest revenue. You can also compete better against larger companies by targeting a niche audience. You will want to include your target audience in your business plan, particularly if you're seeking investors.

Undervaluing What You're Selling

Whether you're selling a product or service, you have to determine an appropriate price that will enable you to make a profit. It can be tempting to undervalue what you're selling to beat out the competition; however, similar to how it is with freelance work, the emphasis has to be on quality rather than price. Customers will pay for quality, and they will come back for more when they know you can produce that high quality.

Skimping on Early Hires

In the effort to quickly fill positions, it's easy to rush the hiring process. That can lead, however, to a mismatch of skills and business needs, bad personality fit with the company culture, and/or lack of commitment to the company's mission. Therefore, before you hire someone to represent your business with clients, be sure you choose the one with the skills you value and the drive to help make your business a success. Remember—they will be making the first impressions with your clients, thus, if that goes badly, it will leave a mark.

There are certainly other pitfalls to look out for, but these are some of the most common ones that cause online businesses to fail. If you can avoid these and surround yourself with people who will give you constructive advice for navigating online business, you will then give yourself a better chance of succeeding.

Chapter Summary

In this chapter, we discussed several common pitfalls that you should avoid to have a better chance of succeeding with your online business. Specifically, we went over the following potential pitfalls:

- Failure to prepare and plan properly.
- Offering a product people aren't buying.
- Ignoring customer feedback and/or not defining your ideal client.
- Undervaluing your product and/or not being unique enough in your business.
- Skimping on hires and underestimating the time you need to make a profit.

[17] https://www.digitalcommerce360.com/article/us-ecommerce-sales/

FINAL WORDS

WE live in uncertain times, but there is still a way you can take more control over your livelihood that doesn't have to be an impetuous response to a crisis. You can take some time to consider whether online or remote work may be right for you, and there are solutions that will work for you, regardless of your level of experience or technological acumen. The coronavirus crisis may be what pushed you into considering this kind of change in your life, but the solution doesn't have to be temporary. You can get into freelance work or open your own online business, and you can decide then, after this pandemic, whether you want to continue with that lifestyle too.

If you ever thought about living life on your own terms, doing something you're passionate about, and taking control of your own destiny, now is your chance to make that a reality. Freelance work is a growing trend, and online businesses are burgeoning, thus you have an opportunity to change your life for the better. The impetus for change may have been a crisis, but you can turn it into an opportunity to change your life fundamentally and take control of your future.

Experts predict that the coronavirus pandemic will permanently change the workforce in at least three ways[18] (Stahl, 2020):

- *More telecommuting*—the remote workforce has already grown 91% over the last decade, and not only with the reality of the coronavirus contagion, but the realization that this could happen again. Therefore, remote work will only become more commonplace. This situation creates enormous opportunities for freelance work and online businesses.

- *Rise in unlimited sick days*—with people being concerned about exposing coworkers to possible contagions, there is likely to be an increase in sick days as more people understand the importance of staying home when they don't feel well. This point would also highlight one of the benefits of online work—you will be less likely to catch anything, and you won't be spreading anything to others either.

◻ ***Increased reliance on tech over travel***—with businesses being forced to use video conferencing rather than commuting, it's likely that technology will see significant bottom-line advantages that will result in permanent changes. This fact thus opens up a whole slew of opportunities for innovative online and freelance businesses. Artificial intelligence solutions and the online businesses to market them can help businesses of every kind make that transition. Telecommunication solutions offer a real alternative to travel, and virtual reality tools can provide employees with training rather than sending them to retreats.

There may be many more changes that will result from this crisis, but just these three represent tremendous opportunities for getting into the online workforce. We may not have asked for this situation, but you can take advantage of it. With the techniques and tips I've given you in this book, you now have the information you need to get started today on a new lifestyle—one in which you can take charge of your own future. In addition, one where you can create the kind of life you've only seen in your dreams. Seize the day, and you can emerge from this crisis with a new life where you call the shots, have more time to spend with your family, and can take time to relax whenever you want. It's up to you now. You can do it, and you are good enough to make it happen. Now, you have the knowledge you need to succeed!

Today is a great day to create your future!

---

[18] https://www.forbes.com/sites/ashleystahl/2020/03/12/3-ways-coronavirus-may-impact-the-future-of-the-workforce/#951e23e1cef5

Leave a Review

I would be incredibly *thankful* if you could take just 60 seconds to write a brief review on Amazon, even if it's just a few sentences.

If you have downloaded the checklist with top ten tips for your daily productivity (the link is at the beginning of the book), you can take a photo, attach it to the review and share your experience. Your success will inspire and encourage many readers who may have difficulties focusing on work and being effective.

Please log into your Amazon account, then find this book *Work from Home During and After Coronavirus*.

Alternatively type this link into your browser or scan the QR code:

amazon.com/review/create-review?&asin=B08CTGH5GM

Customer Reviews

★★★★★ 51

4.8 out of 5 stars ▼

5 star		94%
4 star		2%
3 star		0%
2 star		2%
1 star		2%

Share your thoughts with other customers

Write a customer review

See all 51 customer reviews ▸

My Other Book You Will Love

References

Adams, R. L. *(2019, March 7)*. **7 Online Business Ideas That Could Make You Rich.** *Retrieved March 27, 2020, from https://www.entrepreneur.com/article/299734*

Beat, T. *(2019, October 13)*. **10 Mistakes to Avoid When Starting an Online Business.** *Retrieved March 29, 2020, from https://infobeat.com/10-mistakes-to-avoid-when-starting-an-online-business/*

Braccio-Hering, B. *(2020, February 13)*. **Remote Work Statistics: Shifting Norms and Expectations.** *Retrieved March 20, 2020, from https://www.flexjobs.com/blog/post/remote-work-statistics/*

Bradberry, T. *(2015, January 20)*. **Multitasking Damages Your Brain And Career, New Studies Suggest.** *Retrieved March 20, 2020, from https://www.forbes.com/sites/travisbradberry/2014/10/08/multitasking-damages-your-brain-and-career-new-studies-suggest/#1a0bb6ce56ee*

Braverman Rega, S. B. B. *(2019, December 14)*. **The highest-paying freelance jobs of 2020 where you can earn $90,000 or more.** *Retrieved from https://www.cnbc.com/2019/12/14/highest-paying-freelance-jobs-of-2020-where-you-can-earn-90000-or-more.html*

C. *(2019, June 18)*. **Start-up Mistakes to Avoid When Starting an Online Business.** *Retrieved March 29, 2020, from https://codersera.com/blog/start-up-mistakes-to-avoid-when-starting-an-online-business/*

Cohen, E. S. M. C. *(2020, March 19)*. **Asymptomatic people without coronavirus symptoms might be driving the spread more than we realized.** *Retrieved March 19, 2020, from https://edition.cnn.com/2020/03/14/health/coronavirus-asymptomatic-spread/index.html*

Contributor, G. *(2017, September 11)*. **5 things to consider before becoming a freelancer.** *Retrieved March 20, 2020, from https://www.thejobnetwork.com/5-things-to-consider-before-becoming-a-freelancer/*

Corcione, D. *(2017, August 2)*. **Freelancing 101: What Every Potential Freelancer Should Know.** *Retrieved March 20, 2020, from https://www.businessnewsdaily.com/5242-freelancer-tips.html*

Darlington, N. *(2020, February 2)*. **Freelancer vs. Contractor vs. Employee: What Are You Being Hired As | FreshBooks Blog.** *Retrieved March 20, 2020, from https://www.freshbooks.com/blog/are-you-being-hired-as-an-employee-or-freelancer*

DesMarais, C. *(2020, February 6)*. **Get More Done: 18 Tips for Telecommuters.** *Retrieved March 20, 2020, from https://www.inc.com/christina-desmarais/get-more-done-18-tips-for-telecommuters.html*

Devaney, E. *(n.d.)*. **How to Work From Home: 20 Tips From People Who Do It Successfully.** *Retrieved March 20, 2020, from https://blog.hubspot.com/marketing/productivity-tips-working-from-home*

Digital Commerce 360. *(2020, March 9)*. **US ecommerce sales grow 14.9% in 2019.** *Retrieved March 28, 2020, from https://www.digitalcommerce360.com/article/us-ecommerce-sales/*

Dishman, L. *(2020, March 11)*. **8 strategies to set up remote work during the coronavirus outbreak.** *Retrieved March 20, 2020, from https://www.fastcompany.com/90475330/8-strategies-to-set-up-remote-work-during-the-coronavirus-outbreak*

Ducharme, J. *(2020, March 9)*. **The WHO Estimated COVID-19 Mortality at 3.4%. That Doesn't Tell the Whole Story.** *Retrieved March 19, 2020, from https://time.com/5798168/coronavirus-mortality-rate/*

Duermyer, R. *(2019, August 9)*. **Becoming an At-Home Freelancer.** *Retrieved March 20, 2020, from https://www.thebalancesmb.com/how-to-become-a-freelancer-1794507*

Elorus Team. *(2019, July 17)*. **Choosing a Pricing Model that Fits your Freelance Business.** *Retrieved March 24, 2020, from https://www.elorus.com/blog/choosing-a-pricing-model-that-fits-your-freelance-business/*

eMarketer. *(2019, February 20).* » US Digital Ad Spending Will Surpass Traditional in 2019 eMarketer Newsroom. *Retrieved March 28, 2020, from https://www.emarketer.com/newsroom/index. php/us-digital-ad-spending-will-surpass-traditional-in-2019/*

Emerson, M. *(2017, January 9).* 17 Steps to Launching a Freelance Business. *Retrieved March 24, 2020, from https://succeedasyourownboss.com/17-steps-launching-freelance-business/*

F., I. *(2020a, January 2).* 18 Best Freelance Websites to Find Work in 2020. *Retrieved March 24, 2020, from https://www.hostinger.com/tutorials/best-freelance-websites*

F., I. *(2020b, January 2).* 18 Best Freelance Websites to Find Work in 2020. *Retrieved March 25, 2020, from https://www.hostinger.com/tutorials/best-freelance-websites*

Farrer, L. *(2020, March 17).* Remote Work Advocates Warn Companies About COVID-19 Work-From-Home Strategies. *Retrieved March 20, 2020, from https://www.forbes.com/sites/ laurelfarrer/2020/03/05/ironically-remote-work-advocates-warn-companies-about-covid-19-work-from-home-strategies/#f82c76b20515*

Francia, L. *(2014, April 23).* 8 Common Freelancing Mistakes You Can Avoid. *Retrieved March 26, 2020, from https://www.lifehack.org/articles/work/8-common-freelancing-mistakes-you-can-avoid.html*

Gillivan, C. *(2020a, March 9).* 68 Best Freelance Job Sites for Getting Clients in 2020. *Retrieved March 24, 2020, from https://millo.co/freelance-job-sites*

Gillivan, C. *(2020b, March 9).* 68 Best Freelance Job Sites for Getting Clients in 2020. *Retrieved March 25, 2020, from https://millo.co/freelance-job-sites*

Guidant Financial. *(2019, November 7).* 10 Tax Advantages of C Corporations. *Retrieved March 24, 2020, from https://www.guidantfinancial.com/blog/10-tax-benefits-of-c-corporations/*

Hamm, T. *(2018, October 31).* Seven Strategies for Working from Home from an Experienced Telecommuter. *Retrieved March 20, 2020, from https://www.thesimpledollar.com/make-money/seven-strategies-for-working-from-home-from-an-experienced-telecommuter/*

Haskins, J. E. *(2019, June 20).* How to Start an Online Business in 8 Steps. *Retrieved March 28, 2020, from https://www.legalzoom.com/articles/how-to-start-an-online-business-in-8-steps*

Howington, J. *(2019, October 24).* The 20 Most Popular Work-from-Home Job Titles. *Retrieved March 20, 2020, from https://www.flexjobs.com/blog/post/20-most-common-work-from-home-job-titles-v2/*

K., K. *(2015, October 9).* How to Set Up an Online Business - Complete Beginner's Guide. *Retrieved March 28, 2020, from http://newinternetorder.com/how-to-set-up-an-online-business/*

Kachan, D. *(2019, May 16).* Psychology in Web Design: Exploring Hidden Influences on Users' Decision-Making. *Retrieved March 27, 2020, from https://www.business2community.com/web-design/psychology-in-web-design-exploring-hidden-influences-on-users-decision-making-02200931*

LegalNature. *(n.d.).* 17 Mistakes To Avoid When Starting An Online Business | LegalNature. *Retrieved March 29, 2020, from https://www.legalnature.com/guides/17-mistakes-to-avoid-when-starting-an-online-business*

Levine, L. *(2019, October 29).* 4 Types of Freelance Clients You Should Avoid at All Costs. *Retrieved March 26, 2020, from https://www.themuse.com/advice/4-types-of-freelance-clients-you-should-avoid-at-all-costs*

Limited, S. H. K. *(2019, September 30).* 15 Best Ecommerce Business Ideas to Start in 2020. *Retrieved March 28, 2020, from https://medium.com/@startupr/15-best-ecommerce-business-ideas-to-start-in-2020-daa28febf1d0*

Maguire, A. *(2019, October 9)*. **Top 6 Problems Freelancers Face (and What to Do About Them).** *Retrieved March 26, 2020, from https://www.businessknowhow.com/startup/top-freelancing-problems.htm*

Miles. *(2020, March 27)*. **Top 10 Online Business Ideas in 2020 – How to Make 10k a Month.** *Retrieved March 27, 2020, from https://www.milesbeckler.com/best-online-business-ideas/*

Moon, A. *(2019, November 4)*. **7 Steps to Starting a Small Business Online.** *Retrieved March 28, 2020, from https://www.entrepreneur.com/article/175242*

Moraes, M. *(2020, January 6)*. **82 Best Business Ideas For Newbie Entrepreneurs [2020...** *Retrieved March 27, 2020, from https://digital.com/blog/best-business-ideas/*

Nastor, J. *(2019, December 12)*. **6 Online Business Models (and How to Get Customers).** *Retrieved March 28, 2020, from https://hacktheentrepreneur.com/online-business-models/*

Patterson, M. *(2014, June 11)*. **How to Be Productive and Stay Sane Working at Home: 7 Success Strategies.** *Retrieved March 20, 2020, from https://www.lifehack.org/articles/work/how-productive-and-stay-sane-working-home-7-success-strategies.html*

PCMag. *(2020, March 20)*. **20 Tips for Working From Home.** *Retrieved March 20, 2020, from https://www.pcmag.com/news/get-organized-20-tips-for-working-from-home*

Pinola, M. *(2016, February 25)*. **Freelancer or Employee: Your Best Arguments.** *Retrieved March 20, 2020, from https://lifehacker.com/freelancer-or-employee-your-best-arguments-1761233384*

Pozin, I. *(2020, February 6)*. **5 Things to Consider If You Think Freelancing Is in Your Future.** *Retrieved March 20, 2020, from https://www.inc.com/ilya-pozin/5-things-to-consider-before-taking-plunge-into-freelancing.html*

Prakash, J. P. D. *(2017, December 8)*. **How to Set Up a Business Entity as a Freelancer.** *Retrieved March 24, 2020, from https://www.fundera.com/blog/how-to-set-up-a-business-entity-as-a-freelancer*

Robinson, R. *(2020a, February 27)*. **78 Best Freelance Jobs Websites to Get Remote Freelance Work (Fast) in 2020.** *Retrieved March 24, 2020, from https://www.ryrob.com/freelance-jobs/*

Robinson, R. *(2020b, February 27)*. **78 Best Freelance Jobs Websites to Get Remote Freelance Work (Fast) in 2020.** *Retrieved March 25, 2020, from https://www.ryrob.com/freelance-jobs/#writing*

Robinson, R. *(2020c, February 28)*. **10 Steps How to Start a Freelancing Business While Working Full-Time in 2020 (and Why You Should).** *Retrieved March 24, 2020, from https://www.ryrob.com/why-freelance-while-working-full-time-and-how-to-do-it/*

Robinson, R. *(2020d, March 13)*. **Infographic: Are You Charging the Right Hourly Rate as a Freelancer?** *Retrieved March 24, 2020, from https://www.ryrob.com/infographic-freelance-hourly-rate-setting-your-price/*

Schäferhoff, N. *(2019, December 21)*. **Online Business Ideas.** *Retrieved March 27, 2020, from https://websitesetup.org/online-business-ideas/*

Staff, T. S. D. *(2020, January 28)*. **The Ultimate Freelancer's Guide: Everything You Need to Know About Getting Jobs, Getting Paid and Getting Ahead.** *Retrieved March 20, 2020, from https://www.thesimpledollar.com/financial-wellness/ultimate-freelancers-guide/*

Stahl, A. *(2020, March 12)*. **3 Ways The Coronavirus Outbreak May Change The Workforce.** *Retrieved March 29, 2020, from https://www.forbes.com/sites/ashleystahl/2020/03/12/3-ways-coronavirus-may-impact-the-future-of-the-workforce/#951e23e1cef5*

Stanford News. *(2009, August 24)*. **Media multitaskers pay mental price, Stanford study shows.** *Retrieved March 20, 2020, from https://news.stanford.edu/news/2009/august24/multitask-research-study-082409.html*

Stanford University. *(2018, October 25).* Heavy multitaskers have reduced memory. *Retrieved March 20, 2020, from https://news.stanford.edu/2018/10/25/decade-data-reveals-heavy-multitaskers-reduced-memory-psychologist-says/*

Stolzoff, S. *(2018, November 2).* The number of freelance workers in the United States is climbing. *Retrieved March 21, 2020, from https://qz.com/work/1441108/the-us-now-has-more-than-56-7-million-freelance-workers-and-they-vote/*

Sun, C. *(2016, March 7).* 10 Mistakes to Avoid When Starting an Online Business. *Retrieved March 29, 2020, from https://www.entrepreneur.com/article/250698*

Truex, L. *(2018, December 17).* How to Start a Resume Writing Service Pros, Cons, and Steps to Helping Others Land a Job. *Retrieved March 28, 2020, from https://www.thebalancesmb.com/how-to-start-a-resume-writing-service-3957645*

Twago, T. *(2016, February 25).* 7 mistakes freelancers should avoid. *Retrieved March 26, 2020, from https://www.twago.com/blog/7-mistakes-freelancers-should-avoid-the-etiquette-guide-for-freelancers/*

Uncapher, M. R., & Wagner, A. D. *(2018).* Minds and brains of media multitaskers: Current findings and future directions. *Proceedings of the National Academy of Sciences, 115(40), 9889–9896. https://doi.org/10.1073/pnas.1611612115*

Upwork. *(2019a).* Freelancing in America: 2019 Survey - Upwork. *Retrieved March 24, 2020, from https://www.upwork.com/i/freelancing-in-america/*

Upwork. *(2019b, November 15).* Sixth annual "Freelancing in America" study finds that more people than ever see freelancing as a long-term career path. *Retrieved March 25, 2020, from https://www.upwork.com/press/2019/10/03/freelancing-in-america-2019/*

Upwork and Freelancers Union. *(2017, October 29).* Freelancers predicted to become the U.S. work-force majority within a decade, with nearly 50% of millennial workers already freelancing, annual "Freelancing in America" study finds. Retrieved March 20, 2020, *from https://www.upwork.com/press/2017/10/17/freelancing-in-america-2017/*

U.S. Bureau of Labor Statistics. *(2019, September 4).* Technical Writers : Occupational Outlook Handbook: : U.S. Bureau of Labor Statistics. Retrieved March 28, 2020, *from https://www.bls.gov/ooh/media-and-communication/technical-writers.htm*

van Doremalen, N., Bushmaker, T., Morris, D. H., Holbrook, M. G., Gamble, A., Williamson, B. N., ... Munster, V. J. *(2020).* Aerosol and Surface Stability of SARS-CoV-2 as Compared with SARS-CoV-1. New England Journal of Medicine. *https://doi.org/10.1056/nejmc2004973*

wikiHow. *(2020, February 6).* How to Start an Affiliate Marketing Business. *Retrieved March 28, 2020, from https://www.wikihow.com/Start-an-Affiliate-Marketing-Business*

WorldOmeter. *(2020, March 19).* Coronavirus Update (Live): 244,364 Cases and 10,007 Deaths from COVID-19 Virus Outbreak - Worldometer. Retrieved March 19, 2020, *from https://www.worldometers.info/coronavirus/*

WP Shastra. *(2020a, March 21).* 10 Best Freelance Websites in the World | 2020. *Retrieved from https://wpshastra.com/best-freelance-websites/*

WP Shastra. *(2020b, March 21).* 10 Best Freelance Websites in the World | 2020. Retrieved March 25, 2020, *from https://wpshastra.com/best-freelance-websites/*

Writing, F. *(2018, April 26).* Avoid These 10 Common Freelancing Traps to Run a More Successful Writing Business. *Retrieved March 26, 2020, from https://www.freelancewriting.com/feature-articles/common-freelancing-traps/*

Zetlin, M. *(2020, February 6).* For the Most Productive Workday, Science Says Make Sure to Do This. *Retrieved March 20, 2020, from https://www.inc.com/minda-zetlin/productivity-workday-52-minutes-work-17-minutes-break-travis-bradberry-pomodoro-technique.html*

Dana Wise

WORK FROM HOME
DURING AND AFTER CORONAVIRUS

2020